Lernkrimi Englisch

Deadly Mistake

Joseph Sykes

Nach einer Idee von Christina Bühler, Maren Ermert, Sandra Schambier und Julia Waldner

compact

Baierbrunner Straße 27, 81379 München
Ausgabe 2018

Redaktion: Helga Aichele
Fachkorrektur: Alison Frankland, Nathalie Russell
Produktion: Ute Hausleiter
Titelillustration: Karl Knospe
Lernkrimi-Logo: Carsten Abelbeck
Gestaltung: EKH Webeagentur GbR, textum GmbH
Umschlaggestaltung: red.sign GbR, Stuttgart; Hartmut Baier

ISBN: 978-3-8174-1954-8
381741954/1

www.compactverlag.de, www.lernkrimi.de, www.facebook.com/lernkrimi

Vorwort

Liebe Leserin, lieber Leser,

sicher zum Lernerfolg – mit Spaß und Spannung! Die Compact Lernkrimis mit ihrer Kombination aus Lektüre und didaktischem Übungsanteil eignen sich hervorragend, um breite Sprachkompetenzen in der Fremdsprache zu erwerben. Der Lerner wird dabei durch die spannende Handlung, das angemessene Sprachniveau und den stetig ansteigenden Schwierigkeitsgrad der Übungen gefördert und motiviert.
Entwickelt nach neuesten Erkenntnissen der Fremdsprachendidaktik, sind Compact Lernkrimis das ideale Medium für einen Lernerfolg im Selbststudium. Durch die kleinen Texteinheiten und den hohen Übungsanteil sind sie aber auch als Unterrichtslektüre bestens geeignet.

So lernen Sie mit Compact Lernkrimis:

- **Mit Begeisterung lernen:** Die packende Krimihandlung motiviert Sie beim Lesen des englischen Originaltextes.
- **Wissen intensivieren und erweitern:** Durch die Kombination aus didaktisch aufbereiteter Lektüre und textbezogenen Übungen testen und trainieren Sie Ihre Sprachkenntnisse effektiv. Vokabelangaben auf jeder Seite unterstützen Sie beim Lesen.
- **Systematisch lernen:** Knüpfen Sie an Ihr individuelles Sprachniveau an und setzen Sie sich eigene Lernziele.
- **Unabhängig sein:** Lernen Sie individuell – wo und wann immer Sie wollen.

Viel Spaß beim spannenden Erlernen der englischen Sprache
wünscht Ihnen

Prof. Dr. Christiane Neveling
Didaktik der romanischen Sprachen, Universität Leipzig

Inhalt

Zu diesem Buch

Karneval in Oxford! Am Rosenmontag feiert Thomas Schmitt mit seinen englischen Kollegen und Freunden eine ausgelassene Karnevalsparty. Doch die Feier endet jäh, als Thomas seinen Boss, Alexander Green, erstochen auf der Straße findet. Vom Mörder fehlt jede Spur, doch alle Partygäste sind verdächtig.
Inspektor Hudson, der gerade in Oxford ist, ermittelt zusammen mit der örtlichen Polizei. Und diesmal ist er selbst tiefer in den Fall verstrickt, als ihm lieb ist ... Wird er den Mörder trotzdem schnappen?

Die Ereignisse und die handelnden Personen in diesem Buch sind frei erfunden. Etwaige Ähnlichkeiten mit tatsächlichen Ereignissen oder lebenden Personen wären rein zufällig und unbeabsichtigt.

1 Coffee and Sauerkraut

The look that the girl gave Thomas Schmitt was almost deadly. She was wearing her blonde hair in a ponytail, bright-red lipstick, and thick, black mascara. Angela Haffner was clearly offended by what Thomas had said. She looked him in the eye and waited for a reply.

An uncomfortable atmosphere filled the room. The group of colleagues looked at each other. Everyone was waiting for someone else to speak.

offended	beleidigt
awkward	*hier*: unangenehm
intern	Praktikantin
to spoil	verderben

It was meant to be a joke, Thomas thought to himself.

But Angela was clearly not amused by the suggestion that she and other Berliners needed to "lighten up and learn how to have a good time". He searched his head for something to say to break the awkward silence.

"Sorry, Angela, I... er... I didn't realize you..."

"It's okay," the young German intern answered. "I know you were only joking, but I get so sick of all the clichés: orderly Germans, no sense of humour and an obsession with punctuality. I thought you would understand? I mean, you're German, too."

Thomas began to answer, but Angela interrupted him.

"Forget it," she said with a sigh. "I'm overreacting. It's been a long day. I shouldn't have said that carnival was childish and stupid. Don't let me spoil your fun."

Thomas and Angela were both employees of Chrimarsan Sauerkraut Ltd. They were standing in the hallway of their office in Oxford among a group of co-workers. Most were putting on their coats and preparing to step outside into the bitter cold of a mid-January Friday evening. Angela was right: it had been a very long day. It was after ten o'clock in the evening and the team had spent the whole day rushing to put together an important sales pitch.

"Well, I think it's a great idea, Tom," said George Ratcliffe, one of the managers. "Fancy dress and German beer – what better way to celebrate your fortieth birthday? So carnival is a big thing for you, isn't it?"

"It's huge," Thomas replied, relieved by George's enthusiasm. "Especially back in Cologne. A huge parade goes through the city on Rose Monday. And because my birthday's on Rose Monday this year, I just thought..."

"It would be the perfect opportunity to celebrate both events together?" George asked, finishing Thomas's sentence.

The ginger-haired Geordie playfully punched Thomas on the arm and smiled.

The other colleagues nodded in agreement and laughed. Thomas was glad that he could rely on George to lighten the mood.

"I can't wait!" said another voice in a camp, excited tone.

It was Ewan O'Brian, the Accounts Manager.

"What should I wear?" he continued.

employee	Mitarbeiter
sales pitch	Angebot (Vertrieb)
fancy dress	Verkleidung
ginger-haired	rothaarig
Geordie	Person aus Newcastle
to rely on sb.	sich auf jmd. verlassen
camp	affektiert, übertrieben
Accounts Manager	Leiter der Buchhaltung

Übung 1: Match-up. Welche der folgenden Wörter gehören zusammen? Ordnen Sie zu!

1. [d] spoil	a) the mood
2. [a] lighten	b) the whole day
3. [c] break	c) the silence
4. [b] spend	d) the fun

"Wear whatever you like," Thomas answered. "I'm sure you could make use of your red trousers. Or your cowboy boots? As long as it's fancy dress, fun and..."

"Fabulous?" Ewan asked. "Oh, don't you worry, Thomas. Whatever I wear, it will definitely be fabulous."

The employees laughed again. It was a typical comment from the Accounts Manager, whose sense of fashion made a decorated Christmas tree look rather dull. Angela, too, was laughing. The uncomfortable moment had passed, and Thomas was happy that his idea had caught his colleagues' imagination.

Now, with their coats zipped up tight, the group moved towards the door and began to stream outside. When Angela Haffner had left the building, Thomas caught George Ratcliffe's attention.

"Thanks for your enthusiasm, George. You managed to rescue me from quite an embarrassing situation."

George laughed, showing his big, white teeth. "No problem."

"I'm still learning the rules of office politics. I've only been here for four months. It's different to the German branch."

dull	eintönig
branch	*hier*: Zweigstelle

"Yes, but you've spent those four months as Marketing Manager. In a position like that, politics really matter."

It was true, and Thomas knew it. His **objective** was to **persuade** the Brits that sauerkraut was the new fish and chips. To be successful, he first had to create a comfortable working atmosphere and gain his team's trust.

"Aren't you coming with us?" George asked when he saw that Thomas had no coat on. "You've put in enough hours this week."

"I need to add the final details to my presentation, I'm afraid. I just want to get it finished. Alexander won't be happy if it's late."

objective	Ziel
to persuade	überzeugen

"Well, don't stay too long. It's not good for you."

"I won't," Thomas replied, then said goodbye to his colleague.

As he walked back to his desk, he breathed a sigh of relief. George had believed his lie. He hated lying to him, but it was the only way.

Übung 2: Question tags. Wie lautet das korrekte Frageanhängsel?

1. It's different from the German branch, 1 ______________ ?
2. You're coming, ______________ ?
3. It will definitely be fabulous, ______________ ?
4. I've worked long enough, ______________ ?

Back at his desk, Thomas switched off his computer without doing any more work. He picked up his briefcase and headed straight to Alexander Green's office.

"Can I offer you a coffee or dessert, madam, sir?" the waiter asked.
Inspector James Hudson smiled at the beautiful woman sitting opposite him. There was a low-burning candle between them.
"Raphaela, it's your decision."
"The desserts look very appetizing, but I'm so full after the lasagne, I don't think I could manage one," the woman answered. "Do you fancy a coffee, James?"
"Yes, I think I do. I'll have an espresso, please," Hudson said to the waiter.
"Make that two," the woman added with a charming smile.
It had been a very enjoyable meal, and a perfect first date. Even so, part of Hudson's mind was still on the job, thinking over the details of a case he was currently investigating. He hated the fact that his mind always turned back to work, even on a delightful evening like this. Miss Paddington, his housekeeper, was always telling him that he needed to switch off more often. He usually replied that being switched on around the clock was part of his job. But, he knew, if ever there was a time to put work to one side, it was this evening.
He had met Raphaela on the Internet after creating a profile on the lonely hearts section of the London Times website. At first, he had been sceptical about such a modern approach to dating. However, he became much more optimistic after

to head straight to	direkt zugehen auf
ϟ to fancy sth.	Lust auf etw. haben
lonely hearts section	Kontakt-anzeigen

lecturer in neuroscience	Dozentin der Neurowissenschaften
forward	*hier*: vorlaut
to make it	es schaffen
strand	Strähne
modest	zurückhaltend
to exceed	übertreffen

chatting to Raphaela, a **lecturer in neuroscience** at Oxford University. She had shown only positive qualities over the Internet – intelligence, a good sense of humour and a strong personality. And she had a certain *je ne sais quoi* which Hudson had looked forward to discovering on their first date.

The waiter arrived with the coffees and left the pair to enjoy their final drink of the evening.

"I hope you don't think I'm being too **forward**," Raphaela said, taking a small sip from her cup, "but it would be lovely to see you again, James. Will you be able to **make it** to Oxford again soon?"

Her bright-green eyes seemed to shine with excitement, and she brushed a **strand** of her dark-brown bob behind her ear.

Hudson gave a **modest** smile. He had had high expectations of the date, and Raphaela had more than **exceeded** them.

Übung 3: Placing restaurant orders. Ergänzen Sie die Bestellungen mit den angegebenen Verben!

have make like may

1. I'd ________ the apple pie, please.
2. Please ________ I have the mushroom soup?
3. ________ that another white wine, please.
4. I'll ________ a cappuccino, please.

"I'll make sure that I come back soon. How about next weekend?"

"That's just what I was going to suggest," Raphaela smiled. "There's a play at the Pegasus Theatre that I'd really like to see. Would you be interested in going?"

to pretend	vorgeben
to hail a taxi	ein Taxi heran-winken
text message	SMS

Hudson pretended to think for a second, then replied, "It's a date."

The two finished their coffee and Hudson paid the bill.

Outside, he hailed a taxi for his date, gave her a small kiss on the cheek, and wished her a safe journey home.

Then he took out his mobile phone. There was a new text message from his colleague and friend Elvira Elliot:

Übung 4: Texting language. Lesen Sie weiter und ergänzen Sie die fehlenden typischen SMS-Vokabeln.

2 1 C u

"So, James, did date dr Elvira's advice come in useful? Hope **1.** ________ decided on the grey shirt. The brown **2.** ________ is SO last decade. Hope the charm I taught u was useful **3.** ________!! **4.** ________ u soon. Elvira."

Hudson smiled. It certainly was useful, Elvira, he thought to himself, and took a taxi back to his hotel.

"Looking for me, Thomas?" Alexander Green called as he was walking down the corridor towards his office.

"Is everything okay?"

The UK Manager of Chrimarsan Sauerkraut was a tall man with tidy blond hair and classic good looks. He liked to demonstrate his high salary with his sense of style: he always wore designer suits and had an endless collection of silk ties. His extraordinary confidence made him perfect for his job.

"Yes, everything's fine, Alex. Do you still want to go for a drink? I've finished the presentation, but I can wait for you."

"That's good of you, but I'm going to be here for another hour. Let's go for a drink next week instead. I owe you one for all the work you've put in recently."

In that case, Thomas thought, you owe the whole team a drink. Everyone has worked extremely hard.

salary	Gehalt
to owe	schulden
to curse	fluchen

"Okay," Thomas replied. "Have a nice weekend, Alex."

"Oh, Thomas, one last thing. I was just in Ewan's office, looking for some files, and I couldn't help but overhear your conversation with George. Why did you tell him that you needed to finish the presentation? You've just told me that it's finished."

Thomas cursed himself. It was a stupid idea to lie! Especially when the light was on in Ewan's office and the door was wide open.

He hesitated. He could not tell his boss the truth, which was that he had not wanted to tell his colleagues that he planned to go drinking with the boss. They would say he was sleeping with the enemy.

"Oh, I... I still have one or two small changes to make," Thomas replied. "But that can wait till Monday morning, I'm sure."
Alexander smiled and nodded, and the two men wished each other a nice weekend.

Übung 5: True or false? Welche Aussagen sind korrekt? Markieren Sie mit richtig ✔ oder falsch – !

1. Alexander Green spent a lot of money on his clothes. ❐
2. Alexander suggested going for a drink another time. ❐
3. When Alexander was in Ewan's office, Thomas was talking to Angela. ❐
4. Thomas had to make some changes to his presentation. ❐

As Thomas prepared to leave, a young woman entered the office. She was wearing jeans and a thick, brown coat. Although her black hair was hanging over her face and hiding her eyes, he was convinced that he knew her.
It immediately became obvious that the woman was softly crying and holding a tissue over her nose. When she noticed Thomas, she tried to hold back her tears.
She wiped her eyes and began to cough.
"Are you okay?" Thomas asked. "Can I help? Have you..."

convinced	überzeugt, sicher
obvious	offensichtlich
softly	*hier*: leise

"I'm fine!" the woman protested in a Slavic accent. "I just had a nosebleed on my way to work."

Now Thomas remembered why her face was familiar. She was one of the cleaners, a Polish woman who came some evenings to prepare the office for the next working day.

"Your nose looks really..."

"I'm fine!" the woman cried, louder this time. "Just leave me alone."

Her sobs were returning, and Thomas felt awkward yet again.

"I'll get you some clean tissues," he answered, and walked into the office kitchen.

When he returned, the young cleaner had calmed down slightly. She had pulled her hair away from her face, revealing big blue eyes and clear, pale skin. She thanked him for the tissues. Then, when she moved her hands away from her nose, Thomas realized that she was hiding much more than a nosebleed: her nose was bright red, and her left cheek was cut. This was no nosebleed. It was an injury.

"Your cheeks!" Thomas exclaimed before he could stop himself, and the young woman broke into tears again.

"Oh, Jesus! Soon the whole world is going to know! Is it that obvious? Please don't tell Mr Green. I don't want him to know."

sob	Schluchzen
slightly	ein wenig
to reveal	enthüllen
pale	blass
to exclaim	(aus)rufen

"No, of course I won't tell him. I promise."

"It was Trevor, my husband. He's still out there. He's been at the pub all day and... I didn't mean to make him angry."

"Your *husband* did this to you?" Thomas's eyes were open in shock. "But... why?"

Übung 6: Prepositions. Lesen Sie weiter und ergänzen Sie die fehlenden Präpositionen!

- | on | after | of | of | to

"It wasn't serious when it started. Hurtful comments, telling me my cooking was **disgusting** or that I was fat and ugly. Then shouting and **swearing**. Then I used **1.** ______ arrive home **2.** ______ work in the early hours **3.** ______ the morning and find he had left the children **4.** ______ their own. They're practically babies! And when he came back **5.** ______ home, he always stank of alcohol. He asked me where I had been, and accused me **6.** ______ being **unfaithful**."

She looked at Thomas with fear in her eyes. He took her hand and squeezed it.

"And then he started to hit me. Slap me. Punch me. Kick me. It didn't matter if the kids were there or not. They saw it all, and they still see things now. I want to leave him so much, but where can I go? My parents and two brothers returned to Poland last year."

"I know it sounds scary to be alone with two small children," Thomas said, "but there are people who can help."

"Two small children? There'll be three by the end of the summer!"

disgusting	widerlich
swearing	Fluchen
unfaithful	untreu

The woman placed her hand on her stomach and sighed. "Listen, I'm sorry. You don't need to hear all of this. We're practically strangers..."
Thomas squeezed her hand again.
"There's no such thing as strangers: they're just friends you haven't met yet. I'm Thomas Schmitt."
The woman gave a small smile. "Agnieszka Longley. But most of you Brits have problems with that, so you can call me Aga."
Thomas laughed. "Oh, I'm not British. I'm German. But let's not get into that now. I've had enough of it for one day."
The pair spent another twenty minutes talking before Aga decided that she really needed to get to work. The new friends said goodbye, and as Thomas left, he noticed snowflakes beginning to fall. He headed down the street towards his car.
Seconds later, his mobile phone rang.
"Hello, darling."
"Don't call me 'darling'!" Debbie, his girlfriend, replied in a voice that was part playful, part serious. "You said you'd ring hours ago."

awful	furchtbar
to be abused	misshandelt werden

"Debbie, it's been the day from hell. I lied to my best friend at work, had a secret rendezvous with my boss, and then came across a Polish cleaner who is being beaten by her husband."
Thomas was not sure how he expected Debbie to respond to this, but he was surprised by the concern in her voice.
"Beaten? Thomas, that's **awful**. What the hell? Who is she?"
"Just a cleaner at work. But listen, she asked me to keep quiet about it. She doesn't want anyone to know."
"Thomas, if that girl's **being abused**, she might need our help!" Debbie's tone was deadly serious.

"Listen, darling, I'll explain tomorrow. I'm at my car now, and I want to drive home before I freeze to death. I love you."

Thomas hung up and climbed into his car. The snow was now falling heavily to the ground, covering Oxford's historic streets in a sheet of white. He started the engine, pulled out into the road and drove home through the winter wonderland.

Übung 7: Word spiral. Erraten Sie die umschriebenen Begriffe und tragen Sie sie in die Wortspirale ein!

1	2	3	4	5	6
20	21	22	23	24	7
19	32	33	34	25	8
18	31	36	35	26	9
17	30	29	28	27	10
16	15	14	13	12	11

1-5: These come out of your eyes when you cry.

5-11: The soft front part of the body below the chest.

11-18: Having an important connection to the past.

18-24: A person responsible for keeping a place clean and tidy.

24-30: To say something as a reaction.

30-36: A familiar name for someone you love.

miracle	Wunder
performance	*hier*: Leistung
glance	Blick
incident	Vorfall
to suggest sth.	*hier*: hindeuten auf

A month later, on a dull Monday afternoon in February, an icy wind was still blowing across the south of England.

The atmosphere was just as icy in the conference room at the Chrimarsan Sauerkraut headquarters, where a general meeting was taking place. It was Rose Monday, the most important day of festivities in the Rhineland, and it was Thomas's birthday, too. Alexander Green, however, was not interested in having fun or celebrating with his employees.

"I didn't expect miracles, but these results are... are...," the manager paused for a second, "simply too bad for words. This performance is unacceptable. I want to know who is responsible."

While Alexander was still speaking, Angela Haffner raised her hand. She was possibly the only person in the room with as much self-confidence as Alexander. She had something to say, and she was going to say it.

"Yes, erm...," Alexander began.

"Angela," she said, helping her boss. "I'd just like to say that I understand what you're saying, Mr Green. But I don't feel the team can reach its potential without the introduction of certain changes to the management of the marketing department."

As she said the last few words, she threw a cold glance in Thomas's direction. Ever since the incident a month earlier, the young intern had been acting strangely towards him. But Thomas could not believe what he was hearing now.

Neither could Alexander, his reaction suggested.

"Sorry," he said, looking Angela directly in the eye, "but if I wanted the opinion of a schoolgirl, I'd ask for it."

The room fell silent, and none of the thirty or so employees in the meeting moved a muscle until Alexander began to speak again.

"Your Marketing Manager does an excellent job, and I will not hear otherwise. You interns, however, don't work half as hard as those we had last year. People like you, Matthew," he said, pointing at a man in his mid-twenties, "need to get off your arse and get selling!"

A small laugh came from Ewan O'Brian, who was sitting directly next to Alexander.

"I don't know what you think is so funny, Ewan," Alexander continued, fixing Ewan with an icy stare. "If you think this issue is restricted to sales and marketing, then you're wrong. The IT department's slow reaction to broken computers has been a problem more than once in the past few weeks. This has slowed down the team and has consequently led to late deliveries and complaints from our customers!"

Then, to Thomas's horror, Alexander turned towards him.

"Is there anything you'd like to add to that, Thomas?"

Thomas felt the eyes of everyone in the room turn towards him, and his cheeks began to burn red.

"Er...," he muttered while he quickly looked down at the notes before him, searching for the information he planned to share.

Finally, when he began to speak, the words came out all wrong. Thomas usually spoke English like a native, but at that moment, the language had never been more foreign.

IT	Informations-technik
delivery	Lieferung
complaint	Beschwerde
cheek	Wange
to mutter	murmeln
native	Einheimischer

Übung 8: Correct the mistakes. Lesen Sie weiter und korrigieren Sie die vier Fehler im folgenden Absatz!

"I'm going introduce a new system to deal with any issues you may have. The system steal needs to be checked, and I'll send anyone an e-mail with more details next wick."

1. ______________________ 3. ______________

2. ______________________ 4. ______________

"Thank you, Thomas," Alexander said. "I look forward to that. Everyone else should pay close attention to Thomas's advice. If people fail to do that, I'm afraid heads will start rolling."

Nobody was safe from Alexander's anger, Thomas realized. Except himself. But surely he was the obvious prime target? He could feel and understand his colleagues' frustration at being criticized while he, the Marketing Manager, got off scot-free.

Slowly, the meeting came to an end. Everyone looked rather uneasy, and Thomas felt mentally exhausted. He shut down his computer and headed for the exit. Leaving work early to prepare for his party was an easy way to escape the tension in the office.

prime target	klare Zielscheibe
to get off scot-free	ungeschoren davonkommen
tension	Spannung
failure	*hier*: Reinfall

But would his guests bring this tension with them? Thomas wondered. Would the atmosphere at the party be just as icy? Thomas almost regretted organizing the party. Maybe it would be a failure. Maybe the whole thing was a big, stupid mistake.

2 Captain Green and the German Jester

By 7:30 that evening, Thomas had cleaned his flat, blown up two packets of colourful balloons, and attached these to the walls. Traditional carnival hits **blasted out** from his speakers. A pan of chicken curry was keeping warm on his gas cooker. Standing next to it was enough rice to feed a small army. A series of salads and snacks stood on the kitchen table. And right in the centre was the most important food of all: a big bowl of sweets, toffees and chocolates; the traditional **treats** of the Rose Monday parade.

For the first time since the meeting, Thomas began to relax.

My guests will be in a good mood after a few glasses of Kölsch, Thomas told himself, and he put a few more bottles of the German beer in the fridge. He only hoped the Brits were more **impressed** by German carnival and Kölsch than they were by sauerkraut.

Now the only thing left to do was change into his pirate costume. A white shirt was hanging in his wardrobe together with a long, red **waistcoat** with gold buttons and a pair of brown trousers. A long plastic sword, an **eyepatch**, and a clip-on gold earring completed the costume.

"Aye, aye, cap'ain," Thomas said out loud with a smile.

He was about to get changed when he heard the phone

to blast out	dröhnen
treat	Leckerei
impressed	beeindruckt
waistcoat	Weste
eyepatch	Augenklappe

apologetic	entschuldigend
to make sb.'s life a misery	jmd. das Leben zur Hölle machen
to sigh	seufzen

ringing. It was his home phone, so he knew there were only two possible callers: his mother, calling from Cologne, or Debbie, his girlfriend. Everyone else called him on his mobile.

"He-allo?" Thomas answered, in a mix of English and German.

"Hi, Thomas," came Debbie's voice at the other end.

"Hi, Debbie. Are you on your way?"

"No, I'm not," Debbie said in an apologetic tone. "I'm so sorry, Thomas, but I don't think I can make it to the party. It's just that..."

"What?! What do you mean, Debbie? You *have* to be here!"

"It's Pete. He came round to mine this afternoon and, stupidly, I let him in. Then he just wouldn't stop talking. I tried to make him leave but he wouldn't. He got so angry! He really believes I might take him back. Of course I won't, but I feel so exhausted now. I'm sorry, honey. I really am."

Thomas's mood sank once again. Debbie, the most important person in his life, was unable to make it to his fortieth birthday party. But how could he be angry with her when her ex-boyfriend, Pete, was making her life a misery?

He sighed. "Debbie, the party won't be the same without you. Please, come. You can't let Pete ruin your life like this. The party will help you forget about..."

Thomas was interrupted by the sound of his doorbell.

"Someone's at the door. I'll ring you back in two minutes, okay?"

Thomas was surprised to hear the doorbell ring so early. He had told his guests to arrive from 8 p.m., and it was not yet 7:45.

He opened the door and was surprised again – this time by the face that greeted him.

Übung 9: Odd one out. Welches Wort ist das „schwarze Schaf"? Unterstreichen Sie!

1. chicken curry | beer | toffees | rice
2. wardrobe | earring | waistcoat | eyepatch
3. come | leave | go | forget
4. tense | miserable | sorry | impressed

"Thomas, mate. Happy Birthday!" Alexander Green said with a smile.

He shook Thomas's hand and embraced him with his left arm. Thomas was so shocked by Alex's sudden intimacy that he almost jumped back in surprise. Where was the angry character who had ruled the conference room that afternoon?

"Hi, Alex. Come in!" Thomas said after a couple of seconds.

ϟ mate	Kumpel
intimacy	Vertrautheit
headdress	Kopfschmuck
pigtails	Zöpfe
to burst out laughing	in Gelächter ausbrechen

There was a second person standing about a metre behind Alex, a pretty woman who was waiting to be introduced. Thomas guessed she was in her mid-thirties. She was wearing a brown dress under a brown leather jacket, sandals, a headdress with large white feathers and two stripes of red face paint on each cheek. Her brown hair was tied into two pigtails.

"Hi, I'm Thomas," the young German said, offering her his hand.

"Hi," the woman replied. "I'm..."

"Pocahontas!" Alex cried, and burst out laughing.

out-of-character	ungewöhnlich
sober	nüchtern

Now Thomas realized why his boss was acting so out-of-character. Alex had been drinking. He was not totally drunk, but he certainly was not sober.

The woman gave Alex an unimpressed look with her green eyes. "I'm Raphaela Otterburn," she said. "Pleased to meet you."

"Please come in, both of you. Let me take your coats."

The pair walked into the hallway and handed their jackets to Thomas. Then Thomas realized something else strange – or far too normal. Alex was not wearing a costume, but the same designer suit and electric-blue tie that he had worn to work that day.

"I hope I'm not the only one in fancy dress," Raphaela commented.

"Oh, no, not at all," Thomas answered. "I was just about to get changed into my pirate costume."

Übung 10: Unscramble the dialogue. Lesen Sie weiter und bringen Sie den Dialog in die richtige Reihenfolge!

a) "I can't be the only one without a costume," Alex said.

b) "Well, that's what they've told me."

c) "Really? Everyone?"

d) "Your what?" his boss asked.

e) "Pirate costume. And everyone else is dressing up."

1	2	3	4	5

"Don't worry," Thomas said. "We're more or less the same size. You can borrow the jester costume I wore to carnival last year. What do you think? It should fit you, no problem."
"Oh, I don't know, Thomas. A *jester*? Do you really think that's a good idea? Yes, this is a party. But I'm the manager and it's important my employees remember this. They can't see me as the office idiot, Thomas. Not after today."
Oh no, Thomas thought. The party hasn't even started and already the meeting from hell has been mentioned.
"No," Alex continued, "I really don't think it is a good idea. But if I heard you rightly, you said you have a pirate costume. I don't see a problem with that. Do you, Raphaela?"
Raphaela looked uncomfortable. "I don't really know if..."
"What do you think, Thomas? Captain Green? Yes. I think I'll try it on for size."
How rude! Thomas thought. It seemed that after a few beers Alex Green had no idea how to behave. But this was no time for conflict.

jester	(Hof-)Narr
uncomfortable	*hier*: unbehaglich
to choose to ignore sth.	etw. nicht hören wollen

"It's on my bed, in there," said Thomas, pointing to his bedroom.
Alex did not notice Thomas's annoyed and sarcastic tone of voice, or he chose to ignore it. While he was walking into Thomas's room, the doorbell rang again.
"Excuse me," Thomas said to Raphaela with an awkward smile.
"Happy Birthday, Tom!"
It was his favourite Geordie, George, dressed in an army officer's uniform.
"I hope I'm not too early," George said. "It only took quarter of an hour to get here."

proper officer	waschechter Offizier
to mingle with the guests	sich unter die Gäste mischen
to range from ... to	reichen von ... bis
wizard	Zauberer
reminder	Erinnerung

"Hi, George! It's fine, come in. Alex is already here with a friend. Your costume is great, mate. The jacket, the hat. A proper officer, George!" Thomas smiled.

He then lowered his voice and added, "I'm glad the military is on stand-by. After this afternoon, you never know when things might explode."

Two hours later, the party had really come to life. Thomas was wearing the jester costume his boss had refused to put on. Alex was clearly in love with his image as a pirate. He was mingling with the guests and showing off his clothes. At first, Raphaela had stood quietly on her own, but soon George began speaking to the young Native American. Now the two were laughing and joking as if they had known each other for years.

Most of the guests were Thomas's colleagues, but there were also a few neighbours, a couple of friends from Cologne who lived in London, and some friends he knew through Debbie.

The kitchen, hallway and living room were filled with a variety of characters ranging from Superman, cowboys and a group of wizards, to schoolgirls, witches and nurses.

Matthew Horner, the youngest of Thomas's colleagues, had even arrived in a pair of lederhosen.

"I thought I would try to make you feel at home on your birthday," he had told Thomas.

Thomas had almost replied that the shorts were not traditional in his region, but decided the safest thing to do was smile and laugh. Don't spoil the atmosphere! he kept telling himself.

After a few beers, he stopped giving himself such reminders. He was feeling fine, and so were his guests.

Übung 11: Translation. Lesen Sie weiter und fügen Sie die englische Übersetzung ein!

Ewan O'Brian had kept his **1.** Versprechen ________________. His **2.** Kostüm ____________ was indeed 'fabulous', and much, much **3.** übertriebener __________ than Thomas had ever expected. The accounts manager was dressed in **drag**; a gold **4.** Kleid ____________ and matching gold stiletto shoes, false **5.** Fingernägel ______________ and false eyelashes, red lipstick and a huge, **6.** lockig ____________ blond **wig**.

But it was Angela Braun who offered the biggest surprise of the evening. The young Berliner had obviously changed her mind about carnival and made a real effort with her costume.

"More military!" Thomas said when she finally arrived.

She was wearing a thick **camouflage** jacket and trousers, big army boots, plus a steel helmet and green face paint.

"I just threw it together at the last minute," she replied **non-chalantly**. "Now let me take this coat off before I boil to death."

The group was drinking, talking and dancing together in Thomas's living room as if they were the best of friends.

ϟ drag	Fummel
wig	Perücke
camouflage	Tarnung
nonchalantly	gleichgültig

Thomas looked around and smiled to himself. The party's a success, he thought. Everyone is here. Everyone except...

under one's breath	leise vor sich hin
to overhear	zufällig mithören
tracksuit bottoms	Jogginghose
ϟ Oi!	He!

"Shit!" he said **under his breath**.

Matthew, the Bavarian for the evening, **overheard** him.

"What is it, Thomas?" he asked politely. "Is everything okay?"

"I completely forgot to phone Debbie back. Excuse me, Matthew. I just need to make a quick phone call."

Thomas went into his bedroom and closed the door, then he took out his phone and dialled Debbie's number.

"Hi, this is Deborah Mitchell," came the voice of the answer phone at the other end. "Sorry I can't take your call. Leave a message!"

"Debbie," Thomas said, "I'm so sorry I didn't ring you back. I..."

The doorbell rang and interrupted Thomas's phone call for the second time that evening.

"Call me back," he said and hung up.

When Thomas answered the door, he was confused for a couple of seconds. The man at the door, who looked about thirty years old, was wearing **tracksuit bottoms**, a white England football shirt, and a baseball cap. The word "Jodie" was tattooed down his right arm.

Thomas recognized the man's face, but he could not think who he was.

I don't remember anyone telling me that he would come dressed as a football hooligan, he thought to himself.

"**Oi**, will you turn the music down? Do you know what time it is?"

Of course! Thomas thought in embarrassment. The man was not a party guest, and he was not wearing a costume. It was his neighbour from the flat below.

"I'm so sorry," Thomas began, "I'll turn it down straight away."
"I'll wait here and make sure you do," the man replied coldly.
Thomas turned and headed towards the living room, passing Alexander and Ewan, who were talking in the hall.
The living room was the liveliest it had been all evening.

Übung 12: **Imperatives. Bringen Sie die Wörter in die richtige Reihenfolge, um Aufforderungen zu bilden!**

1. me back call

   ____

2. down the turn music

   ____

3. a leave tone the after message

   ____

4. as as here can you get quickly

   ____

"Viva Colonia!" his guests sang at the top of their voices, dancing together in a circle.
It did not matter that they only knew two words; the music had recreated the atmosphere of Cologne.
"Sorry, guys," Thomas said, and turned down the volume on his stereo. "Can you sing a little bit quieter? I'm sorry."

at the top of one's voice	aus vollem Hals

His guests did not hide their disappointment, and seconds after Thomas had left the room, someone turned the volume back up.

"Oi! Don't you get the message? Turn it down! **Bloody kraut**, coming here, playing your music. We don't like your type around here. You should go back where you came from."

"Take that back," came a voice from behind Thomas.

"Or else? Do you think you're the hard man, Captain Hook?"

"Oh, just **get lost**. I'm not going to waste my breath."

Alex slammed the door and put his arm on Thomas's shoulder.

"You need another drink," he said in a drunken **slur**, then walked off into the kitchen.

The doorbell was ringing again and Thomas could hear his neighbour shouting and swearing in anger.

ϟ bloody kraut	verdammter Deutscher
ϟ Get lost!	Hau ab!
slur	Lallen
ϟ flavour of the month	die derzeitige Nummer eins
to strut	stolzieren

He turned to Ewan. "Thank God for Alex."

Ewan rolled his eyes and folded his arms.

"It's a great party, Thomas, darling, but I have to tell you something. You might think you're Alexander's friend for life, but in reality you're just his **flavour of the month**. Soon you'll be exchanged for someone else, and then you'll be just another employee at Chrimarsan. I should know. I was in your position once. Now excuse me, I'm going to powder my nose."

Ewan then turned, pulled his handbag up his arm, and **strutted** off. Thomas was left standing alone and astonished.

"Come back, Raphaela!" someone was shouting further down the hallway. "It was a joke! Come on, don't go home."

Alex was **staggering** after his companion, who did not look happy.
Raphaela chose not to reply to Alex, but turned to Thomas.
"Thanks for having me, Thomas. I'm sorry I have to leave but..."
"Come on, Raphaela!" Alex cried. "You're too **sensitive**!"

to stagger	schwanken
sensitive	sensibel
ϟ to go out with a bang	mit einem Bombenerfolg enden

Übung 13: Adjectives. Lesen Sie weiter und ergänzen Sie die fehlenden Adjektive!

fun convincing calm sober drunk

"You're 1. ______, Alex!" Raphaela replied, trying to stay 2. ______. "You're completely out of order. Think about what you said when you're 3. ______. Then you might understand why I want an apology."
Raphaela was not even looking at Alex as she spoke. She walked past Thomas and stepped into the stairway.
"Happy Birthday again, Thomas," she said with a smile that was not 4. ______. "Have a 5. ______ evening. I hope the party **goes out with a bang**."

Half an hour later, in a hotel room in Oxford, James Hudson's mobile phone began to ring. It woke the inspector up immediately. He had been asleep with a book in his left hand and an empty glass of whisky in his right, and now he dropped both objects on the floor.

"Hello," he said, taking the call.

"Hello, James," came Elvira Elliot's voice. "Sorry for calling so late. Did I wake you up?"

Hudson had no idea how long he had been asleep or how late it was. He looked at his watch. The hands showed ten to eleven.

"Not at all, Elvira," Hudson lied. "How are you?"

"Bored to death. I've been at the Oxford **Insurance** Conference all day, then I had dinner with my colleagues. Conversation between insurers is far from exciting. Anyway, are you still in Oxford? If you're not on a romantic date, I wanted to ask you out for a drink."

"That sounds great, Elvira. But I'm really tired. I never knew being on holiday could be so **exhausting**. Raphaela has gone to a party tonight with some of the women she works with, and I'm driving back to London tomorrow. Could we meet there some time?"

"Sure, it'd be a pleasure, James. I need to hear all about your dates and this 'Raphaela' character. I imagine Miss Paddington has been busy asking you questions about her already."

That was true. Hudson's **over-protective** housekeeper had not stopped **interrogating** him. She did not seem happy at the idea that Hudson **had a love interest**, especially because this love interest was not Elvira Elliot. But since he had been on several dates in Oxford, Miss Paddington had had to get used to the idea.

insurance	Versicherung
exhausting	anstrengend
over-protective	überfürsorglich
to interrogate	verhören
to have a love interest	in jmd. verliebt sein

Hudson said goodbye to Elvira and decided to ring Raphaela before he went to bed.

"Hello?" An unfamiliar man's voice answered the phone.
"Hello," Hudson replied. "Could I speak to Raphaela, please?"
"Not possible," the man answered with a drunken slur.

The line had gone dead.	Die Leitung war tot.
to be fast asleep	tief und fest schlafen
cardigan	Strickjacke

"And why's that?" Hudson asked, slightly worried.
"She left a while ago, but it seems she's forgotten her phone."
"Who am I speaking to?" Hudson asked.
"Alexander Green... no, Captain Green!" the man replied. "Don't worry, I'll give Raphaela her phone back tomorrow. I'll tell her you called. Goodbye."
"But can you...," Hudson began, but the line had gone dead.
Hudson felt uneasy. Who was this man? And how did he know Raphaela? Just a friend, or... No. He shouldn't think like that.
He decided to call Raphaela's home number, but he was greeted by her answer phone.
He left a message, asking her to ring him when she was home. Then he lay down on his bed and decided to continue reading his book until Raphaela phoned.
Within five minutes, he was fast asleep.[i]

At around half past midnight, Thomas's last guest arrived. Most of his guests were beginning to leave at the same time, but he was happy to open the door to Aga Longley. She was not wearing a costume, just jeans, a simple T-shirt, cardigan and coat. It did not matter; she looked much happier than she did when Thomas met her a month earlier.

Weitere Wendungen mit dem Adverb **fast** sind:
to stand fast = standhaft sein
to be stuck fast = feststecken
to hold fast to sth.
= (an einer Idee) festhalten

Übung 14: Match up the clauses. Welche Satzteile gehören zusammen? Ordnen Sie zu!

1. ☐ Hudson declined Elvira's invitation...
2. ☐ Elvira was bored...
3. ☐ Hudson felt uneasy...
4. ☐ Hudson could not speak to Raphaela...

a) because he did not know who the man was.
b) because he was tired.
c) because she had left her mobile phone at the party.
d) because she had had a boring evening.

"I'm sorry I'm late," she told Thomas. "I've just finished cleaning the office and I wanted to wish you a happy birthday before I go home. I can't stay for long, though. Trevor's waiting for me at home."

As Thomas took Aga into the kitchen for a drink, Angela and Ewan were putting on their coats and preparing to leave. Alexander was sitting on the sofa, looking very tired.

"It's been fun," Angela told the host as he walked past. "Maybe carnival isn't so bad after all."

host	Gastgeber
bully	Tyrann

"Just a shame about Alexander's behaviour," Ewan whispered.

Angela rolled her eyes.

"He's been staring at me all night," she told Thomas quietly. "I could see the lust in his eyes. It's disgusting. At work he's a bully, and when he's had a drink, he's a dirty old man."

This was something Thomas had noticed, too. Alex had been trying to flirt with some of the other girls as well. Maybe his creepy behaviour explained why his guest, Raphaela, had left so abruptly?

creepy	gruselig
⚡ slut	Schlampe
in an instant	augenblicklich, im Nu
to flick a switch	einen Schalter umlegen

Ten minutes later, most of Thomas's friends had left, and now only Aga and Alexander remained.

"I have to leave now, too," Aga told him. "I should get back home."

She finished her glass of water and put on her coat. Thomas escorted her to the door, called the lift up to his floor, the sixth, and wished her a good night.

"I think it's time you left, too, Alex," Thomas said to the pirate on his way to close the curtains. "I can call you a taxi if you like?"

"We need to talk, Thomas. Man to man," Alex said, slurring his words more than ever. "There's something I need to tell you."

Alex was interrupted by a cry in the street. He stood up and moved towards the window.

Outside the entrance to the building, Aga was arguing with a man. Thomas opened the window and immediately saw who it was.

"You're not my wife! You're a slut!" The man cried. "A slut!"

"No, Trevor!" Aga protested. "You don't understand."

"Don't lie. I knew there was someone. And now I know who. You've led me to him, you dirty slut."

Trevor raised his hand and Aga screamed.

"No, Trevor! Please!"

In an instant, Alex was once again sober, as if someone had flicked a switch in his head.

"Shit, Thomas!" he cried. "Who the hell's that madman?"

Übung 15: Simple past. Lesen Sie weiter und ergänzen Sie die fehlenden Verben im Simple Past!

He **1.** run __________ out into the hall and towards the door.

"Come on!" he **2.** cry __________, and was running down the stairs while Thomas was still putting his shoes on.

The arguing in the street **3.** continue __________ as Thomas **4.** search __________ for his door keys. A mobile phone and some keys with a letter 'R' key ring were lying on the sofa, but his own keys had disappeared. It was only when he **5.** put __________ his coat on that he kicked himself. The keys **6.** be __________ in his coat pocket, the most obvious place of all.

Thomas stepped out of his flat, pulled the door shut, and hurried down the stairs.
He had made it down just two flights when someone stopped him. There, walking up the stairs towards him, was his least favourite neighbour.
"You again?" The neighbour asked, and gave Thomas a sour look. "Is that Polish woman with you? All you foreigners are the same."
"Excuse me," Thomas said, trying to be polite, "but I need to..."

"You and your friends need to shut up, that's what."
Thomas was **exasperated**. "Yes, yes. Just let me past."
"I was going to say something myself, but then I..."

exasperated	aufgebracht
dim	schwach, trüb
ripped	aufgerissen
bunch of keys	Schlüsselbund

"Just let me past!" Thomas shouted, and hurried past the man.
The scene was quiet when Thomas opened the door and stepped out into the cold night air. There was no arguing, no screams and no shouting and swearing. The only sound came from a car engine, racing away further down the street.
Aga and her husband? Thomas wondered. It was probably them, since they were nowhere to be seen.
But suddenly something else caught[i] Thomas's attention: a horrific sight just a few metres from his own two feet.
Alexander Green lay on the ground in a pool of blood. In the **dim** light of a street lamp, Thomas could see his bloodstained shirt, which was now as red as his pirate's waistcoat and **ripped** in several places. Alex was on his back; his eyes were open and staring lifelessly at the sky. His body was still.
Thomas took a step back in shock. He reached into his pocket for his mobile phone, but all he found inside was a **bunch of keys**.
Thomas's hands began to shake and he dropped the keys. He fell to his knees, began to shake Alexander's body, and cried out in horror and fear.

Wendungen mit catch

to catch sb.'s attention
= jds. Aufmerksamkeit erregen
to catch sb.'s eye
= jmd. ins Auge fallen
to catch one's breath
= den Atem anhalten
to catch sb. red-handed
= jmd. auf frischer Tat ertappen

Übung 16: Translation quiz. Übersetzen Sie und enträtseln Sie das Lösungswort!

1. Straßenlaterne _ _ _ _ _ _ □ _ _ _
2. bewegungslos _ _ □ _ _
3. Angst □ _ _ _
4. Motor _ _ _ _ _ □
5. höflich _ _ □ _ _ _
6. Tasche _ _ _ _ _ □ _
7. fluchen □ _ _ _ _
8. Weste _ _ _ □ _ _ _ _ _

Lösung: □ □ □ □ □ □ □ □

3 Personal Ties

In a state of horror and panic, Thomas barely noticed the police and ambulance arrive. He watched, still in shock, as paramedics loaded Alexander's dead body into an ambulance and police officers cordoned off the front entrance to his block of flats. Nosy people in neighbouring buildings appeared at their windows, and several neighbours from his own block had come down to see what had happened.

The man from the flat below his was, however, nowhere to be seen. Didn't he know what had happened? Or was he hiding? It was certainly something to mention to the police, Thomas thought.

"We'll need to speak to you," a young officer called Sergeant Clayton informed Thomas. "The information you provide will be extremely important for our investigations. Your flat will also provide us with key evidence. Is there anybody living nearby that you can stay with for a while?"

"My girlfriend, Debbie. Deborah Mitchell." Thomas replied slowly.

He was shaking rather violently.

personal ties *pl*	persönliche Bande
paramedic	Rettungssanitäter
to cordon off	absperren
nosy	neugierig
to provide	bereitstellen
key	*hier*: zentral, entscheidend
evidence	Beweismittel
to shake	*hier*: zittern
violently	*hier*: heftig

account	Bericht
to buy a story	jmd. eine Geschichte abkaufen

The young officer had acted very sympathetically when Thomas explained how he had found Alex's body. Thomas was relieved that the officer believed his account of events. Either that or he had pretended to buy the story.

"Okay, Mr Schmitt," Sergeant Clayton said. "One of my officers will take you to Ms Mitchell's address. I suggest you try to rest so that you can help us put together a picture of who Alexander Green was. You know, the kind of person he was and what relationships he had with the people around him."

The phrase "what relationships he had" suggested to Thomas that the policeman wanted to know who Green's enemies were. But who were Alexander's enemies?

Thomas was scared – scared that if he began to think of answers to this question, he might never be able to stop.

Übung 17: Unscramble. Ordnen Sie die Buchstaben zu sinnvollen Wörtern!

1. deptern p____________________
2. bringhoue n____________________
3. baumclean a____________________
4. lexymeert e____________________

The digital clock read 08:23 when James Hudson woke up. He had slept for over nine hours and he felt refreshed and awake.

But there was one thing bothering him: he had no missed calls on his phone. Why hadn't Raphaela called?
He searched for her home number and pressed "call". While the phone was ringing, he turned the television on and selected the BBC News Channel.
"Now for a summary of the top story in Oxfordshire this morning," the newsreader was telling local viewers.
"Come on, Raphaela!" Hudson said out loud. "Answer!"
"A man was found dead with several stab wounds last night after attending a colleague's birthday party," the newsreader said in a serious tone.

to bother	stören
stab wound	Stichwunde
to investigate	untersuchen
to appeal for witnesses	um Zeugenaussagen bitten
to grab	greifen
to flash	*hier*: aufleuchten

Hudson sighed. He decided to ring Raphaela again in five minutes.
"Alexander Green, aged 43, the UK manager for..."
Hudson dropped his phone. Alexander Green? Wasn't that the name of the man he had spoken to on the phone last night?
"An employee of Chrimarsan Sauerkraut Ltd., who had hosted the party, discovered the body at around 12:50 a.m. Police have cordoned off both ends of Fieldings Road in the Cowley area of Oxford. Sergeant Clayton of Thames Valley Police said the death was being investigated as murder. He and his colleagues will appeal for witnesses this afternoon."
Hudson's eyes remained on the television screen for a few seconds after the report was over. But when his phone began to ring, he grabbed it straight away.
The name he had hoped for was flashing on the screen.
"Hello?" he said, taking the call.

sb.'s heart sank	jmd. wurde das Herz schwer
suspect	Verdächtiger
victim	Opfer

"Hello, James."
Hudson breathed a sigh of relief. Raphaela was all right. Or at least she was speaking to him: her voice suggested that something was wrong.
"Are you okay? I was beginning to worry about you. I just saw a..."
"I'm fine, James, I'm fine. I just... I'm not sure. I don't know how to say this. I don't think we should see each other any more."
Hudson's heart sank. "What?"
"I think you're a great guy, James. But..." Raphaela was finding it difficult to speak.
Was she starting to cry?
"But why?" Hudson asked.
There were a few seconds of silence. It was a painfully awkward silence, the first he had experienced with Raphaela. He had no idea what to say. As a policeman, he was used to dealing with emotional people – suspects, victims, families of victims... but now he was totally lost for words.[i]

> Der Ausdruck **to be lost for words** beschreibt, dass jemand so überrascht oder erschrocken ist, dass ihm die Worte fehlen.

"Please don't call me or come round, James. I can't see you."
She couldn't hide her sobs any longer. "I'm sorry, James."
Then, with a click, she hung up.
Hudson was left feeling cold and confused. Could Raphaela's strange behaviour be connected to the murder of Alexander Green? The emotion in her voice reminded Hudson of various other cases he had seen over the years: heart-broken wives, emotionally insecure witnesses...

Übung 18: Multiple choice. Welches Satzende ist korrekt? Kreuzen Sie an!

1. When Hudson woke up,...
   a) ❐ it was 8:23 p.m.
   b) ❐ he was not feeling sleepy at all.

2. The newsreader reported that...
   a) ❐ there had definitely been a murder in Oxford.
   b) ❐ Fieldings Road had been cordoned off.

3. Raphaela told Hudson that...
   a) ❐ she thought they should stop dating.
   b) ❐ she was not allowed to see him any more.

4. Raphaela ends the phone call by...
   a) ❐ apologizing.
   b) ❐ asking Hudson not to write to her.

Although both Alexander and Green were common names, Hudson suspected that the murder victim and the man he had spoken to on the phone were one and the same person. After all, loud music was playing when Hudson had spoken to the man – and according to the news, Alexander Green had been at a birthday party.

Hudson had to find out more. Luckily, he knew just how to quickly get his hands on the key information on the murder.

He picked up his mobile phone and rang his boss at Scotland Yard, Sir Reginald.

We go back a long way.	Wir kennen uns schon ewig.
to be in the know	Bescheid wissen
short-staffed	knapp an Personal

"James! Speak of the devil." The Chief Inspector began without so much as a 'hello'.

"Good morning, sir," Hudson replied. "Were you talking about me?"

"I've just been speaking to Sir Fleming, Chief Inspector at Thames Valley Police," Sir Reginald replied. "We go back a long way. I'm sure I've mentioned him before. We've got a case with your name on it."

"Thames Valley?" Hudson asked. "Tell me, sir, does this have anything to do with the murder of a certain Alexander Green?"

Übung 19: Missing nouns. Lesen Sie weiter und ergänzen Sie die fehlenden Substantive!

Headquarters job help days

"Very good, James. I'm glad to hear you're already in the know. Sir Fleming is rather short-staffed, you see, and could do with our **1.** __________. You must know Oxford very well by now. You're always there these **2.** __________. So I told Sir Fleming you're just the man for the **3.** __________. I want you at the Thames Valley Police **4.** __________ as soon as possible. Can you leave London now?"

Hudson gave a slight laugh. "I'm not in London, sir. I'm in Oxford."
"Even better!" the Chief Inspector exclaimed. "Well, what are you waiting for, James? Get to work!"

to chuckle	kichern
genuinely	echt
to stab	stechen
mortuary	Leichenhalle
head	*hier*: Chef, Leiter
forensics	Gerichtsmedizin

At around 9:20, Hudson arrived at the Thames Valley Police Headquarters in the village of Kidlington, five miles north of Oxford. It was a short drive in his Bentley from his hotel, which was in the city centre.
Sir Fleming was waiting at the station to greet him and thanked him for agreeing to lead the investigation. He was a large, wide man, with a long, white beard.
So this is what Father Christmas does during the other 364 days of the year, Hudson chuckled to himself.
"Let me introduce you to Detective Sergeant Barry Clayton," Sir Fleming said, and led him to the sergeant's office. "Sergeant Clayton and his team will be working with you on the case."
"Very nice to meet you, sir," Sergeant Clayton said, shaking the inspector's hand. "It's a pleasure to work with you."
The young police officer, who was a rather short black man, looked genuinely pleased, as if he already knew about Hudson's work.
The two men got to work, and it was not long before Hudson had all of the main details of the crime in his head.
"The body was found outside a block of flats on Fieldings Road in Cowley," the sergeant explained. "The man was stabbed at least six times in the chest. The body is at the mortuary. We haven't heard anything from the head of forensics yet, but it's safe to say

to come forward	sich melden
CCTV	Videoüberwachung
to vandalize	mutwillig beschädigen
mugging	Straßenraub

that this man was stabbed to death. He was dead long before the ambulance arrived."

"What do you know about the victim?"

"He's been identified as Alexander Green, a 43-year-old white male. He lived in Oxford and worked as an office manager. He was a tall man and he was wearing fancy dress. A pirate costume, actually."

"He was wearing a pirate costume?" Hudson asked.

"Yes, sir," Sergeant Claydon replied. "Mr Green had been at a fancy dress party that evening in a flat on the sixth floor of a building near to where the body was discovered. The host was Thomas Schmitt, a German citizen who has been living in the UK since September. Mr Schmitt also discovered the body. No other witnesses have come forward yet."

"Then I think it would be a good idea to begin with Mr Schmitt. What other information do you have?" Hudson asked.

"Unfortunately we can't rely on CCTV for evidence. The only camera in the area was broken. Vandalized, it seems."

Hudson gave a big sigh. Without CCTV, their job would be much more difficult. It was just typical! Cameras uselessly recorded the movements of millions of innocent people across Britain each day, and then, when one could prove to be useful, it was broken.

"Mr Green had two mobile phones in his pockets, a packet of chewing gum and a wallet with £148 in cash," Clayton stated.

Hudson raised his eyebrows.

"£148 and two mobile phones? I think it's safe to say we're not dealing with a mugging, then."

Übung 20: Passive voice. Formulieren Sie die Sätze im Passiv!

1. Sir Fleming greeted Hudson at the police station.

____

2. Thomas found Alex Green's body.

____

3. Two of my friends are hosting the party.

____

4. Has anyone identified the body?

____

"Right, sir. Apart from that, his wallet contained all the usual things: a driving licence, bank and credit cards, several business cards, and a few other items. Oh," Clayton added with a small smile, "there was also a card for Oxfun."

"Oxfun?" Hudson asked.

"It's a strip club in the city. Obviously we don't know if Mr Green was a regular visitor there, but maybe we should look into it."

"And the two phones? One business and one personal?"

"Actually, no, sir. Only one appears to be Green's. We're waiting for confirmation from the service provider. But according to the text messages on the other phone, it belongs to someone called Raphaela."

Hudson felt his chest turn tight. What should he say?! Sergeant

confirmation	Bestätigung

Clayton couldn't find out about his personal connection to the case. It would change everything. He needed to speak to Raphaela first.
Whether she would speak to him was another question, though. He had tried to ring her house phone several times on his way to the police headquarters, but she was not answering.
"A lot of the text messages are from the other phone, so probably from Alexander Green. There are also messages from a sender called James. This James was the last person to ring the phone, at 10:59 p.m., so he may be a possible witness."
Now Hudson was beginning to sweat. What the hell was he supposed to do?
Luckily, Hudson's well-practised poker face hid his thoughts from the young sergeant.
"I'll take care of that," Hudson offered. "Later."
"Very well, Inspector," Clayton replied.
"But now," Hudson said, his voice perfectly calm, "I think it's time for us to pay Mr Schmitt a visit."

Übung 21: Americanisms. Geben Sie die britische Entsprechung der amerikanischen Begriffe an!

1. cell phone ______________________

2. Santa Claus ______________________

3. driver's license ______________________

4. to call sb. ______________________

5. vacation ______________________

Deborah Mitchell's house was a traditional terraced house in Banbury Road, near Oxford University. The morning was turning sunny, but it was a cold day, and frost covered the grass.

The front door opened moments after Hudson knocked.

"Good morning," he said, holding his identity badge up to a small, thin woman in her late twenties. "I'm Inspector James Hudson from Scotland Yard. This is my colleague, Sergeant Clayton. We'd like to speak to Mr Thomas Schmitt."

"Oh, come in," Deborah replied. "We've been expecting you."

Hudson and Clayton followed Deborah through the hallway into a large living room. Thomas Schmitt was sitting in a big leather chair wearing a plain black T-shirt and jeans. His eyes were red, and it was clear that he had not slept well, if he had slept at all.

terraced house	Reihenhaus
to rephrase	neu formulieren
drama graduate	ausgebildeter Schauspieler

After more formal introductions, Deborah left the room to make the officers some coffee, and Hudson began the interview.

"Mr Schmitt, we'd like to ask you some questions regarding Mr Green and the party you held last night."

"I know, Inspector," Thomas replied calmly. "I feel sick inside. I'm so confused. I don't know who did this to Alex."

"So you have no idea who would kill Mr Green?" Clayton asked.

"That's not what I said, Sergeant. I said I don't know who killed him. But who *would* kill him? That's another question."

"Then allow me to rephrase the question," Hudson said. "Who do you think might have had a reason to kill Alexander Green?"

Thomas hesitated and started breathing heavily.

The poor man was genuinely distressed, Hudson thought. Either that or he was a drama graduate from Oxford University.

Übung 22: Correct the mistakes. Lesen Sie weiter und korrigieren Sie die sechs Fehler im folgenden Absatz!

"Its sickening to think I might work with a killer," Thomas said slowly, "but Alex had quiet a few enemys at work. Too say he's unpopular is a understatement. Any of my colleagues hated him."

1. ____________________ 4. ____________________

2. ____________________ 5. ____________________

3. ____________________ 6. ____________________

"Such as who?" Hudson asked, ready to note down the names.

"Well, Angela Haffner, a young German intern. She's very open about what she thinks. She says she's underpaid, overworked, and unappreciated by Alex. At the party she was dressed as a soldier in big boots, army trousers, camouflage, and everything. Anyway, she said Alex had been lusting after her, and she called him a dirty old man. I can see her point: she's only 21."

unappreciated	nicht gewürdigt
to lust after sb.	jmd. begehren

"And who else?" Hudson asked.

"Hmm... Ewan O'Brian, our Accounts Manager. He had a love-hate relationship with Alex. But mostly love, I think. He was jealous of my friendship with Alex."

Deborah walked back into the room and gave the police officers a mug of coffee each.

"Your friendship?" Hudson asked, and took a sip of coffee.
"Maybe that's too strong a word," Thomas said in a doubtful voice. "But he definitely didn't like Alex praising me for my work so much. Alex seemed to praise me more than any of the other employees, and Ewan didn't like that. He always has to be the centre of attention, you see. That wasn't a problem at the party; he came in drag."
He sounded like an interesting character, Hudson thought. In his head, he was ticking off each emotion Schmitt referred to: jealousy, hatred, resentment – all typical motives for a crime of passion.
Thomas continued to speak. He seemed to be thinking carefully about his choice of words.
"There's someone else, too. A much more likely suspect, actually. His name is Trevor Longley, and his wife, Aga, is a cleaner at Chrimarsan. She was at my party, too. When she left, her husband was outside and they started arguing in the street. He was shouting violently, calling her a slut. Alex ran down to stop him from hitting Aga, but I didn't see anything after that. I was rushing to follow Alex. When I got outside, Aga and her husband had already disappeared. And Alex was..."
"I see," Sergeant Clayton said.
"So," Thomas said quietly, "I suggest you speak to Trevor Longley. He should help you. Unless he has blood on his hands, of course."

to praise	loben
to tick off	abhaken
resentment	Verbitterung
prime suspect	Hauptverdächtiger

Hudson found it strange that Thomas had changed his mind so much during their interview. At first, he seemed to have no idea who the killer might be. Now he seemed almost certain that Trevor Longley was the prime suspect.

Übung 23: Word search. Finden Sie im Gitternetz sieben Verben, die Alternativen zum Verb „to say" sind!

S	U	G	G	E	S	T	U	S	B
S	A	T	Y	V	P	H	U	H	C
Q	C	V	Y	B	E	Z	H	O	X
T	E	N	I	E	A	R	G	U	E
E	S	P	R	A	K	T	H	T	R
L	P	I	E	E	P	M	J	A	K
L	E	A	S	K	A	P	E	N	N
O	A	L	L	R	U	C	A	L	L

"Did you notice anything odd about Mr Green's behaviour during the evening?" Sergeant Clayton asked.

"He was quite drunk. That probably explains why he was the way he was towards Angela. And he said something odd to me, too. He said something like, 'I need to talk to you, man to man. There's something I need to tell you.' But he was interrupted by the argument between Aga and her husband. I've got no idea what Alex wanted to say."

odd	merkwürdig
to jot down	(schnell) notieren

Hudson jotted down the information. What secret might Green have wanted to share with Schmitt?

"Can you tell us more about the party itself?" Hudson then asked. "And we'd like the contact details of every guest, too, please."

The officers listened to Thomas while he talked about his party in as much detail as possible, from the costumes and the music to the food and drink. He mentioned two **encounters** with an angry neighbour, first at his flat and then on the stairs.

encounter	Begegnung

"I don't know the man's name, I'm afraid," Thomas said, "but he lives on the fifth floor. He has a name tattooed on his arm in big letters. Jenny? Or Josie? Or... maybe Jodie?"

By quarter to one, Hudson and Clayton had almost finished the interview. Hudson wanted to speak to Trevor Longley as soon as possible, and call in at the pathology lab, too. But most of all, he wanted to see Raphaela. No, he *needed* to see her.

It was Sergeant Clayton who mentioned her name to Thomas.

"One last question for now, Thomas. A mobile phone was discovered in Alexander Green's pocket, and we believe it belongs to someone called Raphaela. You haven't mentioned this name, but do you know who she is?"

Thomas opened his mouth to speak, and then seemed unsure about what to say. A few seconds later, he got his words out.

"Yes, I do. Alex brought her to the party as his guest. How could I forget to mention her? I'm sorry, Sergeant. I don't know the woman well, and she left rather suddenly. I think Alex upset her, but I have no idea what he did or said."

Hudson began to wonder. Was Raphaela Green's date[i] for the evening? Had they argued and ended the date[i] during the party? His questions remained only thoughts, however.

Das Substantiv **date** wird in diesem Absatz in zwei leicht unterschiedlichen Bedeutungen verwendet:
Zuerst bezieht sich **date** auf eine **Person** (Raphaela), die mit jmd. verabredet ist, dann auf die Verabredung selbst, also auf ein **Ereignis.**

Übung 24: Fill in the blanks. Lesen Sie weiter und ergänzen Sie die fehlenden Wörter!

The sound of Deborah's **1.** p________ ringing interrupted the conversation.
"Who is it, Debbie?" Thomas asked his **2.** g________.
Deborah looked at the screen of her little silver mobile with a **miserable** look on her **3.** f________. She stood up and walked out of the **4.** r________ without answering Thomas's **5.** q________.

Thomas turned to Hudson. He, too, looked miserable. "Probably Peter, her ex. He just won't leave her alone. It's because of him that she didn't come to the party. She said she was too exhausted after arguing with him all day long."
"Well, I hope she **sorts things out**," Hudson replied with a small smile. "And please thank her for the coffee. We'll be in touch."
As the two officers walked away from the house and back to the car, Inspector James Hudson felt completely **overwhelmed**. He was used to complicated investigations, and he was used to feeling **clueless**. But this time, for the first time ever, Hudson felt **trapped**. He was trapped in the investigation, unable to escape, because this time he was linked to the crime scene.
He knew that he was walking on thin ice – and it would take only one wrong step for the ice to break.

miserable	elend
ϟ to sort things out	eine Sache in Ordnung bringen
overwhelmed	überwältigt
clueless	ahnungslos
trapped	gefangen

4 Stab Wounds and Bloodstains

"A penny for your thoughts, Inspector," Sergeant Clayton said to Hudson.

The pair were sitting in Clayton's police car outside Deborah Mitchell's house.

"Is that all my thoughts are worth?" Hudson replied sarcastically.

"That depends. Are they going to help us find out who killed Alexander Green?"

"I'm not sure about that. Thomas Schmitt has given us an interesting list of contacts. I'm particularly eager to speak to Mr Longley. I doubt Schmitt himself was involved in the crime. The man was a nervous wreck, but those weren't the nerves of a killer. I think he's in shock."

"I was thinking exactly the same," Clayton remarked. "He doesn't seem like a murderer. But he could gain a lot from this crime, you know. He's the Marketing Manager at the company at the moment and is an obvious candidate for promotion. If Alex Green praised Schmitt so much more than the other employees, the managers in Germany are probably impressed by his work, too. Thomas said the Deputy UK Manager is close to retiring.

A penny for your thoughts.	Ich würde gerne wissen, was du denkst.
eager	begierig
nervous wreck	Nervenbündel
deputy	*hier*: Vize-
to retire	in Rente gehen

to draw conclusions	Schlüsse ziehen
state-of-the-art	hochmodern

So Thomas is the obvious candidate to fill Green's shoes." "But he wasn't the only candidate, surely. There must be other managers in Germany who could do Green's job here in England. We can't draw conclusions too soon. We need to speak to the other employees. The office is closed today, isn't it?"
Clayton nodded. "When I spoke to the deputy manager earlier, she said they were closed for two days. But I requested a list of addresses and telephone numbers of all the employees. She said she'd send the information in an e-mail, which she's probably done by now. Shall I check?"
"Yes, that'd be great."
Clayton pulled a state-of-the-art phone out of his pocket and soon he had his inbox open on the screen.

Übung 25: Synonyms. Finden Sie im obigen Textabschnitt die Synonyme für die folgenden Wörter!

1. clear ______________________
2. to ask for ______________________
3. to find out ______________________
4. modern ______________________

"Ah, here we are: a new e-mail from Elaine Briggs."
Within a few seconds, Clayton was reading out the names and addresses of the employees of Chrimarsan Sauerkraut.
The wonders of modern technology, Hudson thought. He then asked Clayton for Agnieszka Longley's address.

production plant	Fertigungs-anlage
pipe	Rohr
to burst	platzen

"32 Higgs Road, Cowley. That's in the same part of town as Thomas's flat."

"Interesting. Let's drive there now. I need to visit the pathology lab later, but I think we should speak to Mr Longley first. Are you going to use your phone to find his address on the map now, eh?"

"Don't be silly," Clayton replied with a laugh. "I've got a satellite navigation system built into the car. Right, let's go!"

Clayton was a fast driver. Hudson had noticed this on their journey to Deborah Mitchell's house. He drove as if every journey was in response to an emergency call. That kind of driving reminded Hudson of someone else... but who?

At that very moment, his mobile phone began to ring and provided him with the answer: Elvira Elliot.

"Hi, James," the young insurance investigator said in a friendly voice. "I just wondered if you're still free tonight for a drink?"

"I wish. I'm afraid not, Elvira. I've been called into an investigation in Oxford. I'm not sure when I'll be back in London."

"A case in Oxford? That must be the stabbing? Mr Green, right?"

"Yes, did you see it on the news?"

"No, a colleague told me. I worked with her last year on a case – a case involving Mr Green's company."

"Chrimarsan Sauerkraut?"

"Exactly. There was a flood at the production plant in Oxford. Some of the pipes burst in the evening and thousands and thousands of litres of water went everywhere. The whole place was flooded, and the plant was practically destroyed. It cost them everything."

"Sounds awful," Hudson replied, "but wasn't it just an accident?"

Übung 26: Adjective or adverb? Lesen Sie weiter und unterstreichen Sie die richtige Variante!

"The circumstances were very **1.** suspicious / suspiciously . The company's UK branch was an **2.** absolute / absolutely failure. They wanted to pull out of the country altogether. But nobody would buy the plant. They **3.** simple / simply couldn't find a buyer. And then the place was **4.** complete / completely flooded. Imagine the insurance payout! It was just what they needed. The **5.** whole / wholly thing seemed **6.** extreme / extremely convenient. Something seemed **7.** wrong / wrongly ."

"And was it?" Hudson asked.
"Not in the end, no. We couldn't prove anything with certainty. Maybe it was just an accident. Anyway, Chrimarsan got back on its feet and they reorganized the management structure."
"And they brought in Thomas Schmitt from Germany."
"Schmitt?" Elvira asked.
"He was the host of the party. Alexander Green was murdered on his doorstep. This flood could be significant, you know, Elvira."
"In that case, let's cancel that drink for the moment. I think

convenient	praktisch, passend

we've got some work to do first. Business before pleasure."
"I can find out about the flood from your company, Elvira. You don't have to take the time to..."
"Don't be ridiculous, James! I'm not missing out! I'll be in Oxford this afternoon."

Business before pleasure.	Erst die Arbeit, dann das Vergnügen.
I'm not missing out!	Ich lass mir das nicht entgehen!
exception	Ausnahme
pushchair	Kinderwagen

From the outside, Agnieszka Longley's house looked very different to Deborah Mitchell's. All of the houses in the street were grey and in need of renovation. The Longley house was no exception. In front of the house was a small garden, where most of the grass and all of the plants were dead. A broken pushchair lay next to a pile of dirty children's toys.
Hudson and Clayton stepped around the objects and knocked on the front door. A minute later, Hudson noticed the curtain behind the front window move slightly. A woman was behind the curtain. She was trying to see the men without being seen herself.
Hudson walked over to the window, knocked on the glass and held up his identity badge.
"It's the police, Mrs Longley," Hudson said.
Moments later, the front door opened a few inches. Hudson was still unable to see the woman's face.
"I'm Inspector James Hudson. This is my colleague, Sergeant Barry Clayton," Hudson introduced them. "We'd like to speak to Mr Longley. Is he in?"
"He's at work," the woman replied. "You can't speak to him."
"In that case, we'd like to speak to you, Mrs Longley," Clayton said. "Could we come in, please?"

"My husband doesn't allow strangers in the house."
"Mrs Longley, this is police business," Hudson added.
After a few seconds of uncertainty, Aga Longley opened the door. Hudson could see that the woman had a black eye, which was either fading or masked by make-up. Her thick black hair hung over her face as if she was trying to hide from the world outside.

Übung 27: Match-up. Welche der folgenden Wörter gehören zusammen? Ordnen Sie zu!

1.	☐ identity	a) door
2.	☐ police	b) business
3.	☐ front	c) eye
4.	☐ black	d) badge

"Inspector Hudson," she said quietly, "you don't know my husband. You don't know what he will do if..."
She stopped and closed her eyes. "I just don't want him to come back and see you here. He wouldn't be too happy."
Hudson paused for a second.
"Mrs Longley, we'll be very discreet. We'll need to speak to your husband, too, but we won't tell him everything you tell us. You needn't worry about that. Please, let's discuss this inside."
Aga nodded, then allowed the two men into her home and closed the door quietly behind them.

black eye	blaues Auge
to fade	verblassen
to mask	verbergen
discreet	diskret

wrist	Handgelenk
to set off	losfahren
to crash	verunglücken

Aga showed them to the living room, which stank of cigarettes and beer. Once Hudson had explained the reason for their visit, she remained silent.

"Your help and cooperation are extremely important to our investigation," said the inspector.

"I heard about it on the news," Aga replied with a sigh. "Mr Green's death was the main story."

"Can you please explain what happened when you left Thomas Schmitt's house last night, Mrs Longley?" Hudson asked.

"My husband didn't kill Mr Green," she replied.

Her tone of voice had changed; she was suddenly extremely defensive. "We... we argued in the street. He wasn't happy. But he didn't touch Mr Green."

"Mrs Longley," Hudson said, "may I remind you that you are speaking to the police."

"I know," Aga replied, "and I'm telling the truth. We were walking back to the car. Trevor was holding my wrist very tightly. Then someone shouted out my name. I turned and saw Mr Green on the doorstep to the block of flats. Trevor pulled me towards the car. The pushing and pulling wasn't nice, Inspector, but he didn't hit me. Then he pushed me into the back of the car and closed the door. He got into the front and set off. While he was driving, he was shouting and swearing like a madman. I was scared – I thought we were going to crash. But we didn't. We got home safely."

"Mrs Longley, may I remind you again that..."

Titel und Berufsbezeichnungen wie **Inspector** werden im Englischen nur groß geschrieben, wenn es sich um eine direkte Anrede handelt oder sie als Teil eines Namens verwendet werden, z.B. **Inspector Hudson.** In allen anderen Fällen werden sie klein geschrieben.

Übung 28: Verb forms. Lesen Sie weiter und ergänzen Sie die fehlenden Verbformen!

Aga **1.** interrupt ______________ Hudson. "I **2.** want ______________ to help you, Inspector, so I **3.** tell ______________ you the truth. My husband can sometimes **4.** be ______________ a violent man. But he **5.** not be ______________ a murderer. And that, Inspector, is the truth."

Hudson **6.** find ______________ the woman's **conviction** quite **astounding**.

Her husband was clearly a **thug** and she could not hide this. But she spoke with great confidence. It was remarkable how this **timid** woman could be so convincing, he thought.

conviction	Überzeugung
astounding	erstaunlich
thug	Schläger(typ)
timid	ängstlich
warehouse	Lagerhaus
industrial estate	Industriepark

But Hudson wasn't fully convinced. Longley was a prime suspect. He and Clayton had to speak to the man himself.

"Where does your husband work, Mrs Longley?"

"He works for Oxford Cameras Direct in the **warehouse** on the North Oxford **Industrial Estate**. But you won't find him there today. He's making some deliveries and will be out all day."

"In that case we'll call in and see him tomorrow," Hudson said.
Aga nodded without smiling. She did not protest or try to convince Hudson not to meet her husband. But it was clear she was scared.

bun	*hier*: Haarknoten
escapade	*hier*: Abenteuer, Streich
Let's get down to business.	Kommen wir zur Sache.
to hospitalize	*hier*: krankenhausreif schlagen

The pathologist was nothing like any of the others Hudson had met during his time working as an inspector. Hudson was used to working with his good friend Tony Barrington, a young, skinny forensic scientist with thick black glasses. Today he was greeted by an Indian woman in her fifties with black hair that was pinned into a bun.
"Mallika Soni," the woman said and shook the inspector's hand. "It's a pleasure to work with you. Tony's told me a lot about you."
"Tony? Tony Barrington?" Hudson asked.
"Oh yes," Mallika replied with a smile. "Tony tells me about all your escapades. But I'm sure you're not here to talk about that, Inspector. Let's get down to business."
The main piece of evidence was now right before Hudson's eyes: Alexander Green's naked dead body.
"He was stabbed six times," Mallika stated.
There was no need to tell him; Hudson could count the wounds for himself.
"We can say for sure that the killer didn't just want to injure or hospitalize Mr Green," the forensics expert continued. "He, or she, wanted to kill him."
"And the weapon?" Hudson asked.

"It hasn't been found, but I'm almost certain it was a small knife. The stab wounds aren't very deep, but they were deep enough to do fatal damage to his internal organs."
Hudson thought back to his conversation with Thomas Schmitt. Three other men had come dressed as pirates. It would have been easy to bring a knife hidden in such a costume. Or easy to steal a knife from Thomas's kitchen? That was another job for the list: he would ask Thomas to write down a list of the knives in his kitchen, then an officer could check to see whether any were missing.

bruising	Bluterguss
sample	Probe

"What else can you tell me?" Hudson asked.
"Two things caught my eye when I examined the wounds. First, I found a couple of small feathers, covered in blood. Second, it seems someone applied pressure to one of the wounds because there is some bruising around it."
Mallika pointed out the light blue area around the stab wound.
"This is where I found the feathers. I believe they fell onto this wound during or after the attack."
"And the blood?" Hudson asked. "Is it all Green's? Or did the killer conveniently leave us a sample?"
"Patience, patience, Inspector," the pathologist told him. "We won't have the test results for a while. As soon as they arrive, I'll be in touch."
Hudson said goodbye to Mallika and headed back to his Bentley. He had two voicemail messages on his mobile phone. The first was from Elvira Elliot:
"Hi, James. I won't be in Oxford until this evening. When you've finished for the day, call me and we can arrange something."

Übung 29: **True or false? Welche Aussagen sind korrekt? Markieren Sie mit richtig ✔ oder falsch – !**

1. Mallika Soni reminded Hudson of other pathologists he had worked with in the past. ❒
2. Hudson knew how many times Alexander had been stabbed before Mallika told him. ❒
3. Hudson knew a knife was missing from Thomas's kitchen. ❒
4. Mallika said she would not receive any blood test results. ❒

The second message was from Sergeant Clayton:
"Hi, boss," it began, "I've arranged a date for you with Thomas's not-so-delightful neighbour. His name is Chris Nicholstone. His girlfriend, Jodie Jones, was at home when I called by. She told me her boyfriend will be home from work at about 5:30. I said we'd call back then. I hope that's okay. I also spoke to the forensics team. They're concentrating on the flat now. They told me they found a Swiss army knife in there, but it was clean. Apart from that, there's not much more to report. They're going to continue looking outside for the weapon. Speak to you soon, boss."
Clayton and Hudson had only met that morning, but already Hudson felt comfortable working with the young sergeant. It was clear from Clayton's casual references to Hudson as his "boss" that he felt the same.

not-so-delightful	nicht gerade reizend
casual	locker

to get to the bottom of sth.	einer Sache auf den Grund gehen

It was 4:10 p.m., so Hudson had one hour and 20 minutes before his meeting with Nicholstone. It was exactly the opportunity he had been waiting for: finally a chance to **get to the bottom of** the mystery which was both personal and professional. It was time to find Raphaela.

Übung 30: Crossword. Lösen Sie das Kreuzworträtsel!

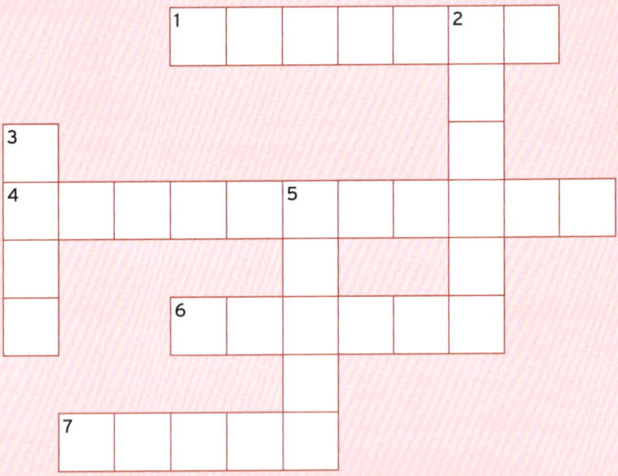

Across

1. Something strange and unexplained, a secret.
4. Cause someone to be taken to hospital.
6. A small amount of substance for a scientist to examine.
7. Another word for injury.

Down

2. End your working life (at the age of 65 in the UK).
3. A violent man.
5. Another word for shy or afraid.

spacious	weitläufig
semi-detached	Doppelhaus-hälfte
brick	Ziegelstein
patio	Veranda
pane	(Fenster-) Scheibe

Hudson tried ringing the young lecturer's home phone number six or seven more times, but there was no answer. He did not want to give up, so he decided to go to Raphaela's house to check whether she was at home.

The house was in Old Marston, at the northern end of the city. It was a nice leafy area full of detached houses with spacious gardens. Raphaela's house was a semi-detached made of red bricks. Her little yellow car was parked in the driveway. Raphaela drove almost everywhere, so this was a sign that she must be at home.

Hudson walked up to the large wooden front door and rang the doorbell. After 20 seconds, he rang it again. He waited again and then rang it a third time.

Come on, Raphaela, open the door! he thought to himself. You might not want to see me, but I need to know you're safe.

When nobody answered the door, he decided to go around the back of the house. There were two large patio doors at the end of the living room and a small patio and garden outside. The tall trees and hedges around the garden created a private little space for relaxation. It was already starting to get dark, and Hudson could hear evening birdsong in the distance.

The glass pane in one of the large patio doors had been smashed, creating a huge hole that was large enough for someone to step through. Had there been a burglary? This was not a good sign.

Slowly and cautiously, Hudson walked up the three small steps onto the patio and stepped through the hole in the door.

"Hello?" he called loudly.

Nobody answered.

"Raphaela?" he asked, louder still. "Raphaela?"

The only noise was the birdsong behind him outside.

Then something caught his eye. At the side of the living room was a big, black **bin bag**. The bag was not full, but it was clear that there was something inside it.

"Hello?" he cried, one last time.

bin bag	Müllbeutel
fabric	Stoff
to jump in shock	vor Schreck zusammenzucken

When nobody replied, Hudson walked across the living room to the black bin bag. He picked it up and rested the bottom in his hand. There was something soft inside – some kind of **fabric**.

Was it a sheet? A dress?

Hudson was now too curious to turn back. He began to shake out the contents.

"No! Let go of that!" came a cry.

Hudson **jumped in shock**.

Raphaela had appeared from nowhere and was running towards him. Before Hudson could react, she was pulling the black bag out of his hands.

To Raphaela's surprise, Hudson simply let go of the bag. She was unable to catch it at once and accidentally turned the bag upside down.

Raphaela put her hands over her face.

"No, no, no!" she was saying, over and over again. "No, no, no!"

"Raphaela, what..."

Hudson stopped abruptly when he saw what had fallen to the floor in front of him.

It was a fancy dress costume of a Native American. And it was completely covered in blood.

5 What Will the Neighbours Say?

"Raphaela?" Hudson said slowly.

The young lecturer did not reply. She stood still with her hands over her face, without saying a word.

"Say something," Hudson said.

But still she did not speak.

"I can't believe what I'm seeing. I can't believe you would... Just tell me it's not true!"

Raphaela lowered her hands from her face to reveal a confused expression.

"Tell you what's not true? What are you suggesting?"

"Your dress is covered in blood, Raphaela! I can see that with my own eyes. Last night you went to a party with a man, and later in the evening that man was stabbed to death. I'm suggesting that I have put two and two together and..."

"And got five!" Raphaela exclaimed. "What the hell, James? You think I killed Alex? Do you really think I'm a killer?"

"Well, explain your behaviour then. The phone call this morning. Not answering your front door. And now! Screaming, grabbing the bag... Tell me what I'm supposed to think."

Raphaela stared at the floor without replying.

"You're doing it again!" Hudson shouted. "Don't pretend this is normal. Don't act as if I'm stupid."

Raphaela said something under her breath, too quietly for Hudson to hear.

alert	wachsam, auf der Hut
figure	Gestalt

"Pardon?" he demanded.

"I'm... scared, James. I was acting strangely because I didn't want you to see me like this. I didn't want *anyone* to see me like this. I feel ashamed."

"So now you're telling me you did it? Jesus, I didn't expect to finish my investigation within a day, and I certainly didn't expect you to..."

"Your investigation?" Raphaela was suddenly alert. "Are you leading the investigation?"

"Yes, Raphaela. I'm caught between two worlds here: private and professional. And to be honest, I really don't know what to do."

"Jesus, James, I can't believe you didn't tell me!" Raphaela cried.

"I promise I can explain."

Now that she knew that Hudson was standing before her as a detective, she was in a state of panic.

"I saw what happened, James. But it wasn't me!"

Übung 31: Prepositions. Lesen Sie weiter und ergänzen Sie die fehlenden Präpositionen!

in after from behind out

"It was a short figure, a man, I think, dressed **1.** ____ a big dark coat and big boots. He was hiding **2.** ____ the wall at the entrance to the building, but I could see him **3.** ____ the street. He stepped **4.** ____ behind Alex. **5.** ____ a few seconds, Alex turned around and saw him, and the man started stabbing him, over and over again."

"Alex fell to the ground and the man just disappeared. He disappeared around the corner and I have no idea where he went from there. And then I..."

Raphaela paused and looked at Hudson.

He had listened carefully to every word she had said, but the more she spoke, the more he doubted her story. Perhaps she could read this in his face now.

"You have to believe me, James. That's what happened!"

"Then why are there bloodstains on your costume? And why do you feel ashamed?"

"I feel ashamed because I didn't do anything to stop it!" she cried. "I didn't scream. I didn't shout. I didn't do anything until it was too late. Only after the man had gone, I ran over to Alex. I knelt down and used part of my dress to try and stop the blood. But it was useless. There was blood everywhere, James. So much blood... And Alex, Alex was..."

Hudson thought back to what Mallika Soni had told him. The feathers on the body. Had Raphaela worn a feather headdress? And the bruising around the wounds from pressure. Raphaela's explanation seemed to fit with the evidence.

"...And then I heard footsteps," she continued. "Someone inside the building was running downstairs. I panicked and ran away. It was a stupid thing to do, I know. But I wasn't thinking straight."

She paused for a few seconds then looked Hudson in the eye. "Do you understand now?" she asked. "Do you understand why I feel so ashamed? I left Alex to die."

Hudson did not know what to think.

the more..., the more...	je mehr ..., desto mehr ...
to kneel down	sich hinknien
to think straight	klar denken

judgement	*hier.* Urteils-fähigkeit
to harass	belästigen
to imply	andeuten

I want to believe you, he thought. I want to believe you so much! But how can I trust my own **judgement**?

"Raphaela," he said, "you need to go to the police. You need to tell them what you've just told me. You can't hide here forever."

"I know," she replied. "But I'm scared they won't believe me. Even you don't believe me!"

"I do believe you," Hudson answered, although he didn't know what he believed. "But I don't understand why you were there at all. Didn't you leave the party two hours before Alex was attacked?"

"Yes. I suppose Thomas Schmitt told you?"

Hudson nodded. He decided not to tell her that he had also spoken to Alex. It was best to keep things simple for the moment...

Übung 32: Compound nouns. Bilden Sie zusammengesetzte Begriffe!

1. ☐	pony	a) dress
2. ☐	head	b) step
3. ☐	foot	c) stick
4. ☐	lip	d) tail

"I left early because I was annoyed. Alex was drunk and acting like an idiot. He spent most of the night **harassing** some German girl dressed as a soldier. Then he **implied** that I might want to sleep with him. And he was being deadly serious. He knew I've got you, and that didn't bother him. I was hurt that he could suggest such a thing."

You've got me? Hudson thought to himself. Not you *had* me? Does that mean we're still together?

Hudson forced himself to concentrate on the investigation. Things were complicated enough without **bringing up** the status of their relationship.

"What happened after you left the party?" he asked.

"I took the last bus home," Raphaela replied. "But when I got home, I realized I'd left my phone and keys at the party. There were no more buses, of course, and I couldn't call a taxi. My next-door neighbours are on holiday and I don't know anyone else on the street, so I decided to walk back towards Cowley. I hoped I would catch a taxi on the way. I never did in the end, so I ended up walking all the way."

Raphaela paused and swallowed. "When I got there, a man and a woman were arguing on the doorstep. I didn't recognize them. The man pulled the woman away, and then I saw Alex appear on the doorstep. He shouted something to the woman and started to run after them."

to bring up	*hier*: zur Sprache bringen
to speed off	davonbrausen

"He ran towards the couple's car?" Hudson asked to confirm.

"Exactly. But he was too slow. The man pushed the woman into the car, jumped into the driver's seat and **sped off** down the road. Alex walked back towards the entrance. And that's when I noticed the man hiding around the corner."

Everything she said made sense. The reason for going back, the timing. It all matched Agnieszka Longley's story, too.

Übung 33: Indefinite pronouns. Ergänzen Sie die fehlenden Pronomen!

anything | anything | something | everything

1. "Any news?" - "No, I haven't heard ________."
2. It all made sense now. ________ was much clearer.
3. Bungee jumping? That's ________ I never want to do.
4. Did you notice ________ strange at all?

"So then when Thomas appeared and you ran away, what did you do? Walk back home?" Hudson asked.

"What else could I do?" Raphaela replied in frustration. "I just wanted to get away from there. And I couldn't get my keys."

Now she started to sob. From their dates, Hudson knew she was a strong, proud woman. But thinking about the previous night's trauma was too much, even for her.

"I was so scared, James," she sobbed. "I was alone in the dark. I was covered in blood and I didn't want to be seen, so I had to take the quiet streets. And I knew there was a madman with a knife out there! I was terrified, James. I've no idea how long it took me to get home. I'm not even really sure how I made it. When I finally got here, I had to break the glass in the back door to get in. I used a rock from the garden. I was so scared that somebody would hear and come round. But nobody did."

terrified	total verängstigt
rock	Stein

Raphaela swallowed again. "Until you arrived. What am I going to do now, James?"

Raphaela continued sobbing. Hudson placed his arm around her neck and pulled her to his chest.

"It's all going to be okay, Raphaela," he said to her, but the words seemed so empty. "You've got to go to the police, though. You do understand that, don't you? The sergeant I'm working with and Chief Inspector Fleming don't know I'm here and, to be honest, I think it would best if we kept our personal lives out of this."

to admit	zugeben

"I know," Raphaela said. "I know inside that I should go to the police. I just don't want to admit that to myself."

"You have to go to them *now*. You can't wait any longer," Hudson said, taking hold of Raphaela's hand.

Übung 34: Unscramble. Lesen Sie weiter und ordnen Sie die Buchstaben zu sinnvollen Wörtern!

It was **1.** reut ______________ that the sooner she came forward, the less she would raise **2.** nissipcou ______________. Plus, it meant Hudson could avoid a very uncomfortable and difficult encounter with her at the police **3.** nostita ______________. His next task was to **4.** erietvwin ______________ Chris Nicholstone, Schmitt's neighbour, so he would be well out of the way.

"You have to give them your dress as well," Hudson added. "It's a **vital** piece of evidence."

Raphaela **wiped** her eyes and nodded.

"Okay," she said. "I will."

Hudson was now convinced that Raphaela was telling the truth. At the same time, he desperately hoped he **was** not **mistaken**.

"I've told you a hundred times!" Chris Nicholstone said, raising his voice. "I was out in the backyard getting some fresh air and escaping the bloody **racket** from the flat above."

"Your answers to our questions may be very useful for our investigation, Mr Nicholstone," Hudson said in a neutral, unenthusiastic voice. "We just want to be one hundred per cent sure that we've understood you correctly."

"I didn't see *anything*!" Nicholstone replied in a **patronizing** tone. "I was in the backyard. That **bloke** got killed outside the front door. I have no idea who killed him. I came back inside through the back door, not the front one, and I didn't see any dead bodies on my way. The only thing I saw was the German guy coming downstairs. He looked pretty stressed, but what's so strange about that?"

vital	entscheidend
to wipe	wischen
to be mistaken	sich täuschen
⚡ racket	Krach
patronizing	gönnerhaft
⚡ bloke	Kerl
packaging	Verpackung(en)

Hudson glanced at Clayton, who gave him a small nod and then noted something down.

They were interviewing Nicholstone and his girlfriend, Jodie Jones, at their flat, which was directly below where Thomas lived. Aga and Trevor Longley's house was like a palace compared to this. Here, there was fast-food **packaging** on the floor, cigarette

burns in the sofa and dust on almost every object in the room.
"Let me turn back to your conversation with Mr Green and Mr Schmitt," Hudson said, addressing Nicholstone. "Were either of the men aggressive towards you at all?"
"Yeah, the dead guy. He told me to get lost, then he shut the door in my face. That's pretty aggressive. But the German bloke wasn't really aggressive. The only thing that bothered me was the music. That was starting to piss me off a lot."
"And you say that you were asleep the whole time, despite the loud music, Miss Jones?" Hudson asked.
"Isn't that what I've said, like, a million times?" the young woman replied.
"I don't know," Hudson replied, equally as sarcastically. "Is it?"

glare	wütender Blick

"Yes, it is," she said with a glare. "Are you going to ask us anything else or not? Because I really want to catch the end of this."
Jodie pointed at the television set and continued to stare at Hudson.

Übung 35: Colloquial English. Ergänzen Sie die umgangssprachlichen Entsprechungen!

1. man ______________________
2. very ______________________
3. to annoy someone ______________________
4. Go away! ______________________
5. noise ______________________

The pair had acted difficultly throughout the interview. Nicholstone looked tired after a long day at work and his girlfriend was annoyed that she was missing her favourite soap opera. However, despite his vulgar mouth and uncooperative nature, Nicholstone did not seem like a killer. And he seemed too stupid to be a convincing liar.

Sergeant Clayton sighed. "Well, Mr Nicholstone, if you think of anything else, please let us know. As I said earlier, it would be useful if you had an alibi."

"An ali-what?" Nicholstone asked.

"An alibi," Clayton repeated. "Proof that you were in the backyard when Mr Green was attacked."

"Ah, okay," Nicholstone said. The confused expression remained on his face.

Clayton and Hudson gave the couple their contact details and prepared to leave. Then, when they were standing at the front door, Nicholstone smiled and turned to his girlfriend.

"Jodie," he said, "shall we give the detective his present now?"

Jodie Jones nodded with a smile, and Hudson wondered what on earth he was talking about. A present?

valuable	wertvoll

Nicholstone headed into the kitchen and reappeared with a plastic bag in his hand.

"I wanted to save the best till last," he said with a slightly crazy smile on his face. "Later in the night, I still couldn't sleep, so I went into the backyard again. And I found this."

He handed Hudson the bag. Hudson looked inside. There was a short, silver knife at the bottom of the bag, covered in dried blood.

"Why the hell didn't you give this to the police before?!" Hudson shouted angrily. "You've been wasting valuable police time!"

puzzled	verblüfft, verwirrt
passageway	Durchgang
to leave one's mark	seine Spuren hinterlassen

"I told you he'd be angry," Jodie said to her boyfriend. "I knew it!"

Clayton took the bag from Hudson and looked inside.

"Jesus Christ!" he exclaimed. "We need to get this to the pathology lab straight away. But how come...?" He looked puzzled.

"What is it, Sergeant Clayton?" Hudson asked.

"Mr Nicholstone, you said you found this in the backyard. If this knife was used to kill Alex Green, how did it make its way from the front door to the backyard?"

Good question, Hudson thought, but he and Clayton were not left wondering for long.

"Er, what about the passageway that runs all the way through the house?" Nicholstone said in a sarcastic tone of voice. "Pretty obvious really, isn't it?"

Of course, Hudson thought, the passageway connected the front and back of the building.

"Okay, Mr Nicholstone," Hudson said with a small nod. "We'll need to take your fingerprints later; you've probably left your mark all over a murder weapon. And I suggest you hand over any evidence a little quicker next time."

"Next time? Does that mean there'll be more questions?"

Hudson did not answer. The knife was an interesting development, but he did not believe Nicholstone was a killer handing over his own murder weapon. That would be too stupid, even for Nicholstone, Hudson thought.

Hudson and Clayton left the man worrying about the questions still to come and stepped out into the stairway.

"Goodbye, Mr Nicholstone," the inspector said and closed the door.

Übung 36: Translation quiz. Übersetzen Sie und enträtseln Sie das Lösungswort!

1. Seifenoper _ _ _ _   _ _ □ _ _
2. offensichtlich _ _ □ _ _ _ _
3. Treppenaufgang _ _ _ □ _ _ _ _
4. Hinterhof _ _ _ _ _ _ _ □
5. wertvoll _ _ _ _ _ _ _ □
6. Geschenk _ _ _ _ _ □ _
7. überzeugend _ _ _ _ _ _ □ _ _ _
8. verärgert _ _ _ _ _ □ _

Lösung: □ □ □ □ □ □ □ □

Clayton shared the news of the knife with the forensic scientists, who were still in Thomas's flat and outside the building. He also asked them to take Nicholstone's fingerprints before delivering the knife to the forensics lab.
It seemed to Hudson that there was plenty of evidence to clear the prime suspects, but nothing to prove anyone guilty. Hopefully the knife would change this.
Back in his Bentley, Hudson checked his mobile phone and noticed that he had a voicemail message from Sir Fleming at Thames Valley Police.

to clear sb.	*hier*: jmd. entlasten

"Hello, Inspector Hudson," the Chief Inspector said. "A potentially important witness has come forward in the Green case: the mysterious Raphaela. Her full name's Raphaela Otterburn, a young woman who was at Schmitt's party. She claims that she witnessed the attack and used her dress to try and stop Green from bleeding. She's handed over the dress and it's on its way to forensics. Can you go and interview her first thing tomorrow morning? Before that, though, I'd like to see you at the station this evening for an update. Is that okay? Call me back."

Hudson began to search for Sir Fleming's number and then changed his mind. He would phone the Chief Inspector, but there was someone else he had to speak to first.

He selected Elvira Elliot's name from his contact list.

"Hi James!" Elvira answered. "Have you finished work now?"

"I've finished my interviews for the day," Hudson answered. "But I have to carry on with them tomorrow, of course."

"And are there any developments you can share?"

"Well, we may have found the murder weapon. A neighbour has handed in a knife he found in the backyard. And an eyewitness has come forward."

"Who?" Elvira asked.

"It's rather complicated," Hudson said. "I should probably tell you face to face. Do you still want to meet? It would be good if you could give me some more background information on the company, too."

to claim	behaupten

Hudson knew he could not hide his relationship with Raphaela from his colleagues forever. They were sure to find out, and he was not looking forward to their reaction. He would tell Elvira, test her reaction and ask for her advice. What was the best way to break this news to Clayton and Sir Fleming?

"Okay, James," she replied. "I've booked into the George Hotel. Maybe we could meet near there?"

"We could just meet in the bar there," Hudson suggested, "then all we have to do is go down a few stairs, both of us."

apparently	anscheinend
severely	heftig
The plot seems so thick.	Der Fall scheint so komplex.

"Oh, you're staying there, too, are you?" Elvira asked, surprised.

"Of course," Hudson replied. "Surely I've mentioned that before?"

"I don't think you have, James."

"It's great," Hudson remarked. "They look after me there almost as well as Miss Paddington does. Right, I'll see you there. I'd better go now. I need to report back to Sir Fleming, the Chief Inspector of Thames Valley Police."

"What time shall I meet you?" Elvira asked.

Hudson paused for a few seconds in thought.

It had been a long day and he still had a lot of work to do in the days to come. But with Elvira's help, the investigation would hopefully go faster.

Hudson still had to interview those employees of Chrimarsan Sauerkraut who apparently severely disliked, or even hated their boss. Did someone hate Alex Green enough to kill him?

"Are you still there, James?" Elvira asked. "What time shall we meet? Nine o'clock?"

"Sorry, Elvira, I was a million miles away. Yes, nine's fine."

"What were you thinking about?"

"Oh, nothing in particular. Just that the plot seems so thick with this case that you could cut it with a knife."

Elvira laughed. "That's nothing new either, James. And I really don't think you would want it any other way."

Übung 37: Questions to the text. Beantworten Sie die folgenden Fragen zum Text!

1. On what topic does Hudson want Elvira's advice?

___

___

2. Where does Hudson suggest he and Elvira meet?

___

___

3. What is Sir Fleming's professional title?

___

___

4. Who does Hudson plan to interview the following day?

___

___

6 Downhill Fast

When Hudson returned Sir Fleming's phone call, the Chief Inspector answered the phone in a fluster.

"I'm sorry, Inspector Hudson, but I've had to leave work. Family emergency. I won't be back at the station until tomorrow afternoon at the earliest. Can we meet then?"

Hudson agreed and wished Sir Fleming the best. He did not ask what this "family emergency" was. From Sir Fleming's tone of voice, it seemed rather serious. But there was no point in speculating.

in a fluster	aufgeregt
to speculate	vermuten
plainly	schlicht
new ground	Neuland

A few hours later, he was sitting in the hotel bar with Elvira Elliot, sipping a glass of whisky.

Elvira almost dropped her gin and tonic in shock when Hudson told her who the eyewitness was.

"Raphaela? Your Raphaela?" she asked in disbelief.

Hudson glanced over his shoulder and looked around the bar. He was checking that Elvira's loud reaction had not caught the attention of the other guests. Nobody seemed to have noticed, so he turned back to Elvira.

"Yes, my Raphaela," Hudson said plainly. "I told you things were complicated. I thought I'd seen everything in my career, but this is new ground for me."

"What exactly did she see?"

"She says she witnessed the attack from a distance. She was at the party but left early and forgot her mobile phone and keys, so she returned to Schmitt's flat. While she was walking back down the street, the crime scene was unfolding. She couldn't identify the attacker, but she believes it was a man. Short, dressed in dark clothing and boots. Anyway, when the killer fled, she ran over to Green and used her dress to apply pressure to the wounds."

Raphaela sighed. "The BBC website has got it all wrong in that case. The journalist wrote that Mr Schmitt discovered the body."

to unfold	sich entwickeln
to flee	flüchten
to choke	sich verschlucken

"That's where things get complicated. He did. Raphaela fled the scene in panic when she heard Schmitt's footsteps."

"Oh, I see," Elvira said with a worried expression on her face. "That wasn't a wise move."

"I know," Hudson replied. "And I know what you're thinking. It looks suspicious. Why would an innocent woman who knew the victim flee the crime scene? But I think she's telling the truth, Elvira. I know I haven't known her for very long, but I'd know if she was lying."

"Are you saying that as a detective or as her..."

Elvira was not sure how to end her sentence.

Hudson ignored the fact that the status of his relationship to Raphaela was in question.

"I'm saying that as a detective, but I'm not claiming that it's possible to be completely neutral in this case. I have to inform Sir Fleming, the Chief Inspector, about my relationship to Raphaela tomorrow."

Elvira nearly choked on her drink this time.

"You haven't told the Chief Inspector?" she asked, coughing. "That's withholding information, James! Potentially serious misconduct, surely? You could be fired!"

Übung 38: Prefixes. Verbinden Sie die Vorsilben mit den Wortstämmen!

1. ☐ mis- — a) possible
2. ☐ un- — b) conduct
3. ☐ dis- — c) belief
4. ☐ im- — d) fold

Hudson had expected Elvira's shocked reaction.
"Thanks for reminding me," he said sarcastically. "When do you think I should inform Sir Fleming?"
"As soon as possible! Next time you see him."
"That's tomorrow afternoon, then. If he makes it into the station, that is. He had to leave today for some kind of family emergency."
"And what are our plans for the morning?"
"*Our* plans?" Hudson asked.
"Yes, James. Our plans. I haven't come to Oxford to stand on the sidelines. If you tell the Chief Inspector about the company's suspicious history – the flood – I'm sure he'll let a trustworthy, highly experienced insurance investigator like me assist you in your investigation," Elvira said with a wink.

to withhold information	Informationen unterschlagen
misconduct	Fehlverhalten
to stand on the sidelines	unbeteiligter Zuschauer sein
trustworthy	vertrauenswürdig
wink	Zwinkern

Übung 39: "Make" or "do"? Lesen Sie weiter und ergänzen Sie die korrekte Verbform!

" 1. not ______________ be so modest, hey, Elvira," Hudson said sarcastically. "Very well, then. We need to **2.** ______________ interviewing the Chrimarsan Sauerkraut party guests *our* main priority tomorrow. Schmitt claims Alex **3.** ______________ plenty of enemies among the staff during his time as manager."

"Why 4. not ______________ that surprise me?" Elvira asked.

Hudson smiled. It was good to have Elvira around. They were a strong team when they got to work, and Hudson could rely on her for support whenever things got tough.

Fifteen minutes later, Hudson had given Elvira a full breakdown of the case, so the two moved on to other topics and enjoyed one last drink together. Then they went to their separate rooms and got some sleep before the important day ahead.

breakdown	*hier*: Aufgliederung, Darstellung

Thomas Schmitt could hardly sleep at all. Every time he closed his eyes, he heard voices in his head:

You're just his flavour of the month, Thomas darling.

I could see the lust in his eyes. He's a dirty old man.

You're not my wife! You're a slut.

Do you think you're the hard man, Captain Hook?

unmistakable	unverkennbar
checkout	Kasse
superstore	großer Supermarkt
foul	mies, fürchterlich

And, over and over again, he heard his boss's slurred words: *We need to talk, man to man. There's something I need to tell you.*

What did Alex mean? What did he need to tell him?

Each time Thomas thought the voices had stopped, he turned over in bed and closed his eyes. But each time he did so, a face would appear. In his mind, someone was next to him.

It was Alex Green.

His lifeless face had holes for eyes and a sick but unmistakable smile.

"You'll never find out!" the face said, the lips still smiling.

Wendungen mit time

time and (time) again = immer wieder

for the time being = vorerst, für den Moment

in time = pünktlich

many a time = oft

over time = mit der Zeit

waste of time = Zeitverschwendung

Then, time and again, he would open his eyes and almost jump out of bed in panic. But of course there was no one in the bedroom apart from Debbie and himself.

Thomas was wide awake by six o'clock. There was no point staying in bed now, he thought, so he decided to get up and do the shopping while there would be no queues at the checkout. There was a 24-hour superstore just a couple of miles from Debbie's house on the A40, one of the main roads out of Oxford.

The A40 was fairly quiet. It was mostly delivery lorries on the road.

Still, after a sleepless night, Thomas was in a foul mood.

Übung 40: Antonyms. Finden Sie im obigen Textabschnitt die Gegenteile zu folgenden Begriffen!

1. vanish ________________
2. alive ________________
3. sleepy ________________
4. back alley ________________
5. in good humour ________________

"Hast du keinen Blinker?!" Thomas shouted angrily at the lorry in front of him.

Without **indicating**, the driver had slowed down as if he was going to stop. Impatiently, Thomas pulled out, **accelerated** and began to overtake the lorry. The road went slightly downhill, however, and now the lorry, too, was beginning to go faster again. Thomas had to go even faster to get past the vehicle.

Once he had overtaken the lorry, Thomas pressed the brake pedal. He was fast approaching a set of traffic lights on red.

It was only then that Thomas noticed something was wrong. When he tried to brake, the vehicle did not react. In fact, it was speeding up as the hill became **steeper**: 51 miles an hour, 52 miles an hour, 53 miles an hour...

He pressed the brake again and again, but still the car did not slow down.

to indicate	*hier*: blinken
accelerate	Gas geben
steep	steil

tyre	Reifen
to skid	schlittern
screech	Quietschen
4x4 (four-by-four)	Allradfahrzeug
deafening	ohrenbetäubend
split second	Sekundenbruchteil

The red light was getting closer. "Abbremsen! Abbremsen!" he screamed at his car, pushing down as hard as he could on the brake pedal. 56 miles[i] an hour...

The road was beginning to flatten out and there was a single silver car ahead of him. It was waiting at the red light, about 100 metres ahead.

Thomas pressed and pressed and pressed on the brake pedal but nothing happened. The brakes had completely failed.

80 metres, 50 metres, 30, 20...

Just metres from the silver car, Thomas grabbed the handbrake and pulled it up as hard as he could. A horrific scream came from the tyres and Thomas lost control of the car.

After skidding onto the wrong side of the road and missing the silver car by inches, the car span 90 degrees on its tyres. But it continued to skid, right into the middle of the crossroads. The screech of car and lorry brakes rang out from vehicles all around.

Thomas's car had turned 180 degrees now, although Thomas had no idea where he was any more. When the car finally came to a halt, he did not see a green 4x4 miss him by a metre or so; nor did he see a little blue car brake to a standstill to his right. He did not see the lorry to his left either.

> Das metrische System ist im Englischen nach wie vor nicht in allen Kontexten gebräuchlich. Das traditionelle Längenmaß **mile** (Meile) entspricht 1,6 km.

He did, however, hear the sound of a horn and the deafening scream of tyres. A split second later, everything went black.

Übung 41: Match up the clauses. Welche Satzteile gehören zusammen? Ordnen Sie zu!

1. ☐ The lorry began to accelerate...
2. ☐ The vehicle did not react...
3. ☐ Thomas pulled on the handbrake...
4. ☐ A large car almost hit Thomas's own...

a) when Schmitt was overtaking it.
b) just after Thomas's car had stopped spinning.
c) when the silver car was just metres away.
d) when Thomas tried to brake.

Sir Fleming had not arrived at the station when Hudson called at 8:15, but the Deputy Chief Inspector was happy to give Elvira Elliot permission to accompany Hudson.
Sergeant Clayton was nowhere to be seen outside Ewan O'Brian's address at 9:00, the agreed meeting place and time. Hudson tried to ring the young officer, but the call was **diverted** to an answerphone. At 9:10, with still no sign of Clayton, Hudson and Elvira decided to start without him.
After ten minutes with Ewan O'Brian in his designer kitchen, sipping espresso and eating biscotti, Hudson and Elvira had reached the same conclusion: deep down, O'Brian was not the man he wanted the world to believe he was. Thomas Schmitt had painted a lively picture of the Accounts Manager, and his modern house, complete with

to divert	umleiten

gadget	technische Spielerei
self-assured	selbstsicher

fashionable decor and the latest **gadgets**, suggested that he was a proud, **self-assured** character. But today, O'Brian was neither lively nor self-assured. He was wearing an old orange jumper that looked several sizes too small for him, his hair was a mess, and he was shaking his legs violently. His eyes looked glassy and white.

For the first ten minutes, O'Brian had nervously told the officers how much he was going to miss his boss.

Übung 42: Missing words. Lesen Sie weiter und ergänzen Sie die fehlenden Wörter!

time | hard | way | track | midnight

"What **1.** ________ did you leave Mr Schmitt's party on Monday, Mr O'Brian?" Hudson started to question him.

"A little after **2.** ________? 12:30? I don't know. I lost **3.** ________ of time."

"Think **4.** ________, Mr O'Brian," Hudson said firmly.

"Okay, it was about 12:30, I think. Oh, but I just don't know!"

"Let's put it this **5.** ________, then, Mr O'Brian," Elvira said. "Where were you at 12:50 a.m.? Outside Mr Schmitt's home?"

"It still feels unreal," Ewan O'Brian said, his legs shaking more than ever. "I mean, the idea of Alex gone is just... inconceivable."

Hudson was about to repeat Elvira's question when O'Brian seemed to collect himself. His glassy eyes moved slightly and came to life.

"12:50, you say?" O'Brian asked, returning to Elvira's question. "Oh, back here, most certainly. I was getting ready for bed. My boyfriend, Charlie, picked me up from the party and brought me straight home."

"Could we have a contact number for your boyfriend to confirm this?" Hudson asked.

"There's no need for that," came a voice from behind Hudson and Elvira, taking them somewhat by surprise.

A tall man wearing a pinstripe suit and waistcoat was standing in the doorway. He walked over to Hudson and Elvira and offered them his hand.

"Charlie Collins," he said with a confident smile. "Ewan's other half. I can confirm that I picked him up at around half past twelve and then we came straight back here."

inconceivable	unvorstellbar
pinstripe suit	Nadelstreifen-anzug
ϟ Don't get your knickers in a twist.	Reg dich nicht auf.

"May I ask how long you've been standing there?" Hudson asked.

"Only a second, Inspector," Collins replied wish a shrug. "Don't get your knickers in a twist. I'm about to leave for work. I'm meeting a client in an hour, but I thought you'd probably want to speak to me first. Ewan has been very upset since he found out about Alex. I can probably give you a much clearer picture of how it was than Ewan himself."

"Were you at the party?" Hudson asked. "Because, **with all due respect**, Mr Collins, I think Mr O'Brian is..."

"I'm not talking about the party," Collins interrupted Hudson. "I'm talking about Alexander Green, and what kind of man he was."

"Charlie," O'Brian tried to stop his boyfriend, "just forget about it. It's history now!"

"He played with people's minds," Charlie Collins continued, ignoring him. "Ewan used to **worship** the man. He would do anything for him. But for Alexander it was just tactics."

"Tactics for what?" Elvira asked.

"Tactics to stop Ewan from..."

"That's enough, Charlie!" O'Brian shouted. "Just leave!"

with all due respect	bei allem nötigen Respekt
to worship	verehren
to torture	quälen, foltern
emotional blackmail	emotional unter Druck setzen
to prick up one's ears	die Ohren spitzen

"No, Ewan! That man psychologically **tortured** you and kept you silent. He stopped you from telling the world about his dirty work!"

"Shut up, Charlie!" O'Brian cried desperately. "Alex was a good man! He wasn't perfect, but who is?"

"Alex Green gave you his attention and friendship to stop you telling the truth to the insurance company," Collins replied forcefully. "It was **emotional blackmail**."

Elvira and Hudson **pricked up their ears**.

"What do you...," Hudson began, but Ewan O'Brian interrupted him.

"Enough!" he shouted. "That's it. I won't say another word until I've spoken to my lawyer."

Übung 43: Conjunctions. Ergänzen Sie die Sätze mit den Konjunktionen!

since until while once

1. Charlie was in the room ________ Ewan was talking.
2. The investigation will be easier ________ we know the facts.
3. Elvira did not stop calling ________ James agreed to meet her.
4. Ewan had looked nervous ________ the inspector arrived.

Sergeant Clayton was standing outside with an apologetic expression on his face when Hudson and Elvira left Ewan O'Brian's house.

"I'm so sorry, boss! You'll never guess what kind of a morning I've had. My wife's ill, I was running late, and then my young son decided to give my mobile a bath. After that I..."

"Excuses, excuses!" Hudson said with a smile. "No time for them now. I need you to organize an interview for me: I want Ewan O'Brian and Charlie Collins – his partner in life, and possibly his partner in crime – at the station. This is Elvira Elliot, insurance investigator. She's an old friend of mine, and she's got an interesting theory that we should definitely pursue."

partner in crime	Komplize
to pursue	verfolgen

redundancy payout	Abfindung
foul play	falsches Spiel, Verbrechen
to tie in with sth.	in Verbindung stehen mit
pensively	nachdenklich

"Nice to meet you, Miss Elliot," Sergeant Clayton said.
Elvira smiled politely. "Call me Elvira," she said, then began to present her theory. "Collins made an interesting comment: he said Green had persuaded O'Brian not to tell the truth to the insurance company. I'm sure he was referring to the flood at the Chrimarsan Sauerkraut production plant last year. I believe Alexander Green deliberately caused this flood. The company had been performing so badly in the UK that Green knew he'd be fired if he didn't act. The flood could have signalled a redundancy payout. But it didn't – the company managed to recover from the flood and Green remained UK Manager. O'Brian must have known about the foul play, so Green had to keep him silent. He pretended to be best friends forever to keep O'Brian quiet. Or, more accurately, best friends until it became too tiring. O'Brian then had mixed feelings, loving and hating his boss at the same time."
"This is all very well and good," Clayton noted, "but how does it tie in with Green's murder? Does O'Brian have an alibi?"
"Yes, but only provided by his boyfriend, so it's not worth much," Elvira remarked. "Collins also had every reason to hate Green – he was jealous of the relationship between Green and O'Brian, plus Green was making his boyfriend's life a misery. Collins probably had more reason to kill Green than O'Brian did."
Sergeant Clayton nodded slowly and pensively.
"I see your logic. I'll arrange the interview."
"Great," Hudson said, rubbing his hands together. "We'll meet later for the interviews with George Ratcliffe and Trevor Longley. For now, Elvira and I are going to pay Miss Haffner a visit."

Übung 44: Word spiral. Finden Sie die gesuchten Begriffe und tragen Sie sie in die Wortspirale ein!

1	2	3	4	5	6	7
22	23	24	25	26	27	8
21	36	37	38	39	28	9
20	35	42	41	40	29	10
19	34	33	32	31	30	11
18	17	16	15	14	13	12

1-7: Someone's "other half" is their life ...

7-14: ... Otterburn is a neuroscience lecturer.

14-23: An adjective meaning "sorry".

23-27: The front part of the body below the neck.

27-32: A calculated action to reach a certain goal.

32-36: An illegal act.

36-42: A feeling such as joy, fear or sadness.

"I'm not going to describe him as my best friend just because he's dead," Angela Haffner said bluntly.

"Even so, Miss Haffner, I'm a little surprised at your anger towards Mr Green," Elvira Elliot replied. "Why the bitterness?"

bluntly — unverblümt

"He was a slave-driver," Angela said. "I give the company my all, and what do I get in return? A tiny salary, a bunch of idiots for colleagues, and a sexist, pig-headed pervert for a boss."

to give one's all	alles geben
bunch	*hier*: Haufen
pervert	Perverser
to mistake sb. for sb. else	jmd. verwechseln
to slide	*hier*: schieben
calling card	Visitenkarte

Hudson thought that her honesty illustrated all the motives she might have, but was she cold enough to have killed her boss?

He had already realized that she fitted Raphaela's description of the killer: she was fairly short, and in her dark army costume and big boots, she could have easily been mistaken for a man.

"What time did you leave the party, Miss Haffner?" he asked.

"12:34."

"That's very precise," Elvira said, raising an eyebrow.

Angela took her mobile phone out of her pocket, pressed a button, and then slid it across the kitchen table.

Hudson looked at the screen. It showed a call Angela had received at 00:34 from a contact named "Martin A2B".

"Martin is a driver – my favourite driver – with A2B Taxis," Angela explained. "He always rings me to tell me he's outside waiting. If you ask him, he'll confirm that he brought me straight home from Thomas's place. Here's the number."

She handed Hudson a calling card for A2B Taxis from her purse. The woman would have a watertight alibi if the taxi company was able to confirm her story, Hudson thought.

"Do you have the clothes you wore to Thomas Schmitt's party?" Hudson asked. "Mr Schmitt mentioned an army costume."

Angela stood up and fetched a black bin bag from the other side of the kitchen.

"I knew you'd want that," she said. "It's all in there."
The girl was organized, Hudson thought. Almost too organized.

peculiar	seltsam
to suit sb.	jmd. stehen

"Did you notice anything peculiar when you left?" Elvira asked.
The young girl paused for a few seconds and then smiled.
"Yes, actually. Martin, the driver, had a new haircut. It really didn't suit him, and I told him that. I probably even said, 'Martin, you look peculiar with that haircut.' He wouldn't listen, of course. And then he drove me home, and I was in bed by one. I thought that I would have a normal day at work ahead of me. How wrong was I?!"

Übung 45: Fill in the blanks. Lesen Sie weiter und fügen Sie die englischen Übersetzungen der folgenden Begriffe richtig ein!

Freundin | klingeln | unbekannt | Stimme | Sekunde

At that moment, Hudson's phone began to **1.** ________.
"Excuse me one **2.** ________," Hudson said and walked into the hallway.
An **3.** ________ number flashed on the screen.
"James Hudson speaking."
"Inspector Hudson," a quiet woman's **4.** ________ replied. "It's Deborah Mitchell here, Thomas Schmitt's **5.** ________."

"Hello Deborah," Hudson replied, a little concerned.

"Something awful has happened, Inspector," Deborah said, trying to hold herself together. "Thomas was in a car crash this morning."

"I'm..."

"He's not dead... but he's... he's lucky to be alive."

"I'm so sorry, Deborah. That's..."

"Listen," Deborah said, getting back to the point of her call. "You need to come to the hospital and talk to Thomas. He is convinced it wasn't an accident."

"Sorry?" Hudson asked. "What do you mean?"

Deborah didn't hesitate for a second.

"He thinks somebody tried to kill him!"

7 A Deadly Mistake?

"Thank you for your time, Miss Haffner," Hudson said to Angela with a polite but purely professional smile. "We're very grateful for your time."

On the outside, he was calmly and carefully bringing the interview to an end. But inside he was desperate to share the important news with Elvira. When Angela had closed the front door behind them and they were at the end of her garden path, Hudson turned to Elvira and took a deep breath.

"So, who was on the phone?" Elvira asked just as Hudson was about to speak.

"Deborah Mitchell," Hudson said grimly. "And she wasn't delivering good news at all. Thomas Schmitt has been in a car crash, and it was serious. According to Miss Mitchell, his brakes failed. His car skidded through a red light and was hit side-on by a lorry."

Hudson paused for a second, expecting Elvira to say something, but all she did was stare at him.

"Apparently the fire brigade pulled Schmitt's unconscious body out of the wreckage," Hudson continued. "He regained consciousness at the hospital. If I understand Mitchell correctly, he was very lucky to come away with cuts and bruises. He could have been killed."

grimly	grimmig
unconscious	bewusstlos
wreckage	Wrack(teile)

Elvira shook her head slowly. "That's... amazing."
Hudson nodded his head. "It certainly sounds amazing, yes. But Deborah said something else; something quite worrying, in fact. Schmitt is convinced that it wasn't an accident. He thinks someone **tampered with** his brakes. And he's managed to convince Deborah of that, too."
Elvira's **jaw dropped** wide open. "Schmitt thinks someone tried to kill him? Could that really be true?"
"I don't know," Hudson replied. "On the one hand, the man's in shock and probably very paranoid after Green's murder. And he's a businessman, not a mechanic. On the other hand, is it very likely that the crash was a **coincidence**? It could very well be connected to Green's murder. It's definitely a line we need to follow."
"Of course," Elvira said, now nodding her head enthusiastically.

to tamper with	sich zu schaffen machen an
sb.'s jaw dropped	jmd. fiel die Kinnlade herunter
coincidence	Zufall
mutual enemy	gemeinsamer Feind
intense	*hier*: leidenschaftlich
fraud	Betrug

"If there is a connection, it could mean that Green and Schmitt have a **mutual enemy**," Hudson remarked. "We know that plenty of people hated Green, but I can only think of one person who had something against Thomas Schmitt."
"Ewan O'Brian!" Elvira said almost immediately.
"Precisely," Hudson replied. "When Sergeant Clayton and I interviewed Thomas, he told us that Ewan was jealous of his friendship with Alex Green."
"And now that we've met Ewan," Elvira added, "we know about his **intense** personality. His love for his boss might have caused him to cover up **fraud**. Maybe the jealousy he felt towards Thomas

led to hatred, and hatred led to attempted murder?"

attempted murder	Mordversuch
hint	Spur, Hauch
bombshell	Bombe

"Maybe," Hudson said, "but we don't even know whether the brakes were tampered with or not. Finding out if they were is my top priority at the moment. I'll ask Clayton to order a full forensic report on Thomas's car. And I could do with more concrete details about the Chrimarsan fraud case. Could you get your hands on the full report and summarize the key points?"

"Of course," Elvira said, "it'd be my pleasure."

"Great. I'm going to the hospital now to see Thomas Schmitt."

"Aren't you forgetting an important date?" Elvira asked with more than a hint of sarcasm in her voice. "And I thought you were looking forward to it so much."

"A date? Who with?"

"Sir Fleming! You'll have to save that bombshell for later."

Übung 46: Noun forms. Verbinden Sie die Wortstämme mit den Endsilben, um Substantive zu bilden!

1. ☐ polite — a) -ism
2. ☐ desparat — b) -ness
3. ☐ professional — c) -ion
4. ☐ amaze — d) -ment

When Hudson explained to Sir Fleming on the phone that he was unable to meet, the Chief Inspector was in a bad mood.

in exasperation	verärgert
to snap	*hier*: blaffen
giddy excitement	ausgelassene Freude
anxiety	Sorge

"The key witness is in a major car crash and you have to find out from his girlfriend?!" he exclaimed in exasperation. "Where is the coordination? Why didn't the officers on the scene report to you?"

"To be fair, sir, they couldn't possibly have known about Thomas's connection to the Green murder so soon after the crash."

"Well, they *should* have known!" Sir Fleming snapped in reply. He then sighed and changed the topic.

"What did Raphaela Otterburn have to say for herself when you interviewed her this morning?"

The R-word had previously filled Hudson with giddy excitement. Now, whenever Raphaela's name was mentioned in connection with the investigation, it filled him with uncertainty and anxiety.

Übung 47: Unscramble. Lesen Sie weiter und ordnen Sie die Buchstaben zu sinnvollen Wörtern!

"The **1.** gimint ____________ wasn't convenient for her in the end," he lied to Sir Fleming. "I'll let you know how it goes when we **2.** lifyaln ____________ meet."

"Not **3.** tennnvoice ____________?! Doesn't the woman know we're trying to organize an interview as part of a **4.** rumred ____________ investigation, not a bloody tea **5.** tyrap ____________!"

Hudson wondered if Sir Fleming's foul mood was connected to his family emergency, but he didn't mention this. When he had asked after his family at the start of the conversation, Sir Fleming had given a very vague answer.

vague	vage, ausweichend
Worse things happen at sea.	Es könnte schlimmer sein.
appealing	verlockend
superstitious	abergläubisch
to suspend sth.	etw. aufhängen
plaster	Gips

"It's nothing major. Worse things happen at sea."

Sir Fleming's words stuck in Hudson's mind as the conversation came to an end. *Worse things happen at sea*.

Thinking about his meeting with Sir Fleming still to come, the idea of going down with a sinking ship had never seemed so appealing.

"I promise you, I'm usually very rational," Thomas Schmitt told Hudson when the detective arrived at his bedside. "I'm not superstitious at all. But I just know this wasn't an accident. I just know it. I can feel it."

Schmitt was lying on his back with bandages around both his arms and his forehead. His eyes were even redder than the previous morning and his left leg was suspended in the air in plaster.

The doctor had given Hudson ten minutes to speak to Thomas Schmitt. After that, he had said, Mr Schmitt needed to rest.

"Can you explain what makes you think like this?" Hudson now asked Thomas Schmitt. "What was it that makes you think someone tampered with the brakes?"

"It was so sudden. There were no warning signs that the brakes were faulty. And besides, I keep my car in good condition. Good brakes don't just suddenly fail," Thomas said quietly.

Übung 48: Translation. Übersetzen Sie die folgenden Sätze ins Deutsche!

1. Hudson found the idea of telling Sir Fleming about Raphaela not very appealing.

   ____

2. I broke my leg and it was put in plaster!

   ____

3. I can't make any calls because my mobile is faulty.

   ____

4. I'm not superstitious at all.

   ____

Hudson now had only two or three minutes left to speak to Schmitt. Although the patient was in good health, all things considered, his exhausted face told the full story. He had **had a real brush with death**.

to have a real brush with death	dem Tode knapp entronnen sein

"I don't want to put any pressure on you, Mr Schmitt, but can you think of anyone who might have a reason to tamper with your car?"

"I wish I could say no," Thomas said after a few moments' thought. "But when I think about it, it's obvious. Trevor Longley. God, it all makes sense."

The realization seemed to add to Thomas's pain.

"It all makes sense!" he said again. "Alex and I were both witnesses. Alex must have seen Longley hit his wife, out there in the street, and I...," Thomas gave a long and frustrated sigh.

"What is it, Mr Schmitt?" Hudson asked.

"I think I'm the only one Aga has told. The only one who knows what goes on behind closed doors. Trevor Longley obviously didn't like the fact that I had learnt about his unhappy family affairs. Given the way he treats his wife, is it surprising that he'd try to kill me?"

Hudson thought about what Aga had said: "He's no murderer. And that's the truth." Had she lied for her violent husband?

Hudson heard the door into Thomas's private room open and guessed it was the doctor coming to tell him that his time was up.

"Tom, mate!" came a man's voice – but certainly not a doctor's – from behind Hudson. "Tom, I can't believe it! What the hell happened?!"

Thomas gave a tiny but definite smile. He was happy to see his visitor. Hudson turned to see a slightly **plump** man with ginger hair who was wearing a grey woolly jumper and ripped jeans.

Übung 49: Adjectives. Wie lauten die Steigerungsformen der folgenden Adjektive?

1. rational __________ __________
2. heavy __________ __________
3. fit __________ __________
4. good __________ __________

"Excuse me, sir!" came another voice, and a nurse appeared alongside the ginger-haired man. "I said Mr Schmitt isn't receiving any visitors at the moment."
"But he's my best mate!" protested the man in a Geordie accent. "I need to see for myself that he's all right!"
"I'm fine, George," came Thomas's quiet voice from the bed. "But I'm busy with Inspector Hudson right now. Be patient."
"Inspector Hudson?" the man asked. "Inspector James Hudson?"

plump	mollig
to cope with	zurechtkommen mit
to duly obey	ordnungsgemäß Folge leisten
to drown	ertrinken

"Yes," Hudson replied. "And I'm guessing you're..."
"George Ratcliffe. I've been trying to ring you to say I was coming here, but your phone was turned off. But you're here so I guess that means..."
"I couldn't make it to the interview with you, either," this time Hudson finished George's sentence.
"Exactly."
The nurse coughed to get their attention.
"Gentlemen, I'm going to have to ask you to leave. Mr Schmitt can't **cope with** this stress at the moment."
The nurse was not asking, but telling George and Hudson to leave, and the men **duly obeyed.**
"Do you mind if we do the interview here at the hospital?" Hudson asked.
"Sure," George replied. "Shall we go and grab a coffee?"
"That sounds like a fine idea, Mr Ratcliffe," Hudson replied. "I just need to inform my colleague of this, then we can start."
Sergeant Clayton had sent Hudson a text message to say that he had replaced his phone after it had "**drowned**". Hudson selected

the number and started scratching his head, waiting for an answer.

Übung 50: Verb forms. Lesen Sie weiter und ergänzen Sie die fehlenden Verbformen!

"Hi, boss," said Sergeant Clayton when he **1.** pick ____________ up the phone. "I **2.** be ____________ just about to call you, actually. There's something important you should **3.** know ____________."

"**4.** let ____________ me see: George Ratcliffe wasn't in?"

"Well, that too, but I **5.** not consider ____________ that too exciting. No, I **6.** want ____________ to tell you the news from forensics. First of all, the team looking at the car should be able **7.** give ____________ us a basic picture by tomorrow; they'll have a rough idea of whether there **8.** be ____________ any foul play or not."

"Okay, great," Hudson **9.** reply ____________.

"They've also informed me that only Alex Green's blood – and none of Raphaela Otterburn's – can be identified on the dress. They did find traces of her DNA elsewhere, however: on the feather that was on one of Alex Green's wounds."

"And have you heard from Elvira at all?" Hudson asked, trying to move the conversation away from Raphaela.

"Yes, boss. She told me she tried ringing you but you had turned your phone off. Her colleague, who led the flood investigation, has sent her the final report. She's never read it before, so she's busy collecting any information to support or **disprove** her theory."

"Okay, good," Hudson answered. "Anyway, my original reason for calling was to tell you this: George Ratcliffe is here at the hospital. He came to visit Thomas, so we're holding the interview here. I suggest we meet outside Trevor Longley's workplace – the camera warehouse – at 4:00. What do you think?"

to disprove	widerlegen
to finalize	endgültig ausarbeiten
to get back to sb.	sich wieder bei jmd. melden

"That's fine. I still need to **finalize** the details for the O'Brian and Collins interview, so in the meantime I'll continue working on that. But tell me quickly: does Schmitt have any idea who might have cut his brakes?"

"He seems convinced that it was Longley. He believes that Longley killed Green and tried to kill him, too. But I'm not so sure about that. We certainly don't have enough evidence to arrest the man."

"Let's wait and see[i] what forensics have to say when they **get back to us** about the hair," Clayton said casually.

"Pardon?" Hudson asked. "What hair?"

"Oh, I'm sorry! That's the important thing I wanted to tell you! Forensics found a hair on the knife that Chris Nicholstone gave us yesterday. They're going to take a DNA sample. If the hair doesn't belong to Nicholstone or Green, it may well belong to the killer."

Das Idiom **(Let's) wait and see!** wird oft mit „Abwarten und Tee trinken." übersetzt. Hier ist die Übersetzung „Erstmal abwarten ..." treffender.

Übung 51: Crossword. Lösen Sie das Kreuzworträtsel!

Across

2. To die by being unable to breathe under water.

4. To make a vehicle go more slowly.

6. To force a suspected criminal to attend the police station.

Down

1. To confirm plans and sort out the final details.

2. This contains a person's genetic information.

3. To do what you have been told to do.

5. If you have a ... idea, you don't know all the details.

to devour	verschlingen
the latter	letzteres
↯ hot bit of stuff	scharfe Braut, heißes Gerät
disrespectful	respektlos

George Ratcliffe was waiting for Hudson in the hospital canteen. There were two small plastic cups of coffee on the table in front of him, and Ratcliffe was devouring a chocolate bar.

"Your coffee will be cold, Inspector!" he joked as Hudson sat down.

"I'm sorry, Mr Ratcliffe. I had to make an important call. Now, it would be good if you could tell me everything you remember about Monday night, from the moment you arrived to the moment you left."

"Well, I have to admit that my later memories are a bit cloudy, Inspector," Ratcliffe explained with a smile. "After all, I was at the party to have a good time. And once I'd had a few beers, I was more interested in celebrating with my mates than trying to remember every detail."

Either Ratcliffe was not taking the interview seriously, or he was a very light-hearted man. Hudson believed it was the latter, but Ratcliffe's humorous approach still made the detective suspicious.

"What time did you arrive?" Hudson asked.

Looking at Ratcliffe, he took a sip of his coffee, which looked and tasted awful.

"Just before 8:00 p.m.," Georg Ratcliffe replied. "I was one of the first to arrive. Only the slave-driver – I mean Mr Green – arrived before me, with his date for the evening. She was a hot bit of stuff dressed as an Indian."

"What was your costume?" Hudson asked quickly.

He wanted to move on from Ratcliffe's disrespectful reference to Raphaela.

Übung 52: Fill in the blanks. Lesen Sie weiter und ergänzen Sie die fehlenden Wörter!

"I was a **1.** m __________ officer. I was really glad when Tom said he liked it because I'd put a lot of effort into preparing it, you know. **At the end of the day**, you've got to for big occasions like a fortieth **2.** b __________ party. Unlike Alex Green. He hadn't bothered to organize a **3.** c __________ at all. He couldn't even be **4.** b __________ to hire one. At the end of the **5.** d __________, with a **6.** s __________ like his, you'd think he could afford to hire one, wouldn't you?"

At the end of the day, I'm going to **throttle you** if you use that expression one more time, Hudson thought. But the man had said something which seemed to contradict the crime scene.

"But surely Mr Green was wearing fancy dress? He was found in a pirate costume."

"Oh, but that wasn't his!" Ratcliffe laughed. "Didn't Tom tell you? No, the pirate costume was Tom's. When Green arrived without a costume, he practically stole the pirate costume from Tom's room. So Tom had to wear an old jester costume instead. Don't get me wrong, he looked good. But he should have said no to Alex. It was his birthday. He should have been a pirate. **End of story.**"

ϟ at the end of the day	letzten Endes
to throttle sb.	jmd. erdrosseln
ϟ End of story.	Basta!, Und Schluss.

to target sb.	jmd. ins Visier nehmen
bewildered	verwirrt

End of story, indeed! Hudson thought. It was quite possibly the key piece of information missing from the puzzle.

Had Alexander Green's killer targeted the man in the pirate costume because he thought it was Thomas Schmitt? In that case, Alexander Green's death had been the result of a deadly mistake. Had the killer then tried to kill Thomas again by tampering with his car brakes, and failed for a second time?

He could not be sure, but Hudson was already nodding to himself, unable to hide a confident smile from the bewildered Geordie sitting in front of him. It all made sense now.

Übung 53: Questions to the text. Beantworten Sie die folgenden Fragen zum Text!

1. What was George Ratcliffe doing when Hudson arrived in the canteen?

2. George drank a few beers at the party. What was the consequence?

3. How did George describe Raphaela?

4. Hudson suspects a "deadly mistake" was made - what might this have been?

8 Doctor's Orders

Inspector Hudson scratched his chin. He and Sergeant Clayton were interviewing Trevor Longley, a short, bearded man, in the workers' rest room of the Oxford Cameras Direct warehouse.

"Mr Longley," Hudson began, "two nights ago, you were seen arguing with your wife, Mrs Aga Longley, on the steps outside 7 Fieldings Road, Cowley. Can you confirm that..."

"I don't know what my Agnieszka's been telling you," Longley said in a quiet voice.

He interrupted Hudson, but without any hint of aggression. "She's got an over-active imagination, Inspector. It's useful when she's playing with the kids, but she sometimes forgets where fantasy ends and reality begins."

bearded	bärtig
over-active imagination	lebhafte Fantasie

Had Agnieszka told Longley about her visit from the police, or did Longley suppose she had reported his domestic violence?

In either case, Clayton handled the question with tact. "Mr Longley, I don't know what makes you think we're here today to discuss your wife's imagination. We're not. I want to know where you were at 12:50 in the early hours of Tuesday morning."

Longley appeared suspicious. It was as if he had been fully prepared to answer questions about domestic violence, but not about anything else.

"12:50?" he asked.

He opened his mouth and began to scratch one of his front teeth. "At home, I suppose."

"And how did you get from 7 Fieldings Road back to your house?"

"I drove, of course. I don't know which nosy people reported my argument with Agnieszka, but they must have seen me leave, too. I don't understand what this has got to do with...," he paused. "Actually, what is this all about?"

"Sergeant Clayton and I are investigating the murder of...," Hudson began.

"Murder?!" Longley exclaimed. "Christ! Who's dead?"

Hudson and Clayton glanced at each other. Did he really not know? The murder had been the top local news story for two days.

"Wait a minute," Longley said. "Are you interviewing me as part of a murder investigation?"

"It's a routine procedure to interview all those who were near the crime scene," Hudson said, trying to reassure the man.

"You'll need to interview Agnieszka, too, in that case. She was there when we were arguing, as you know."

He started scratching his teeth again. "She might be able to help."

split personality	gespaltene Persönlichkeit

"Thanks," Hudson replied, confused by Longley's reaction. Did the man really not realize that they had already spoken to his wife? Did the fact that they were interviewing him not ring alarm bells in his head at all?

Was Trevor Longley, with his quiet, relatively calm voice, a simple thug with a split personality, or the cleverest suspect of all?

Übung 54: If-clauses. Ergänzen Sie die fehlenden Verbformen!

1. "If he isn't the murderer, then who be ___________?"
2. I tell _______________________ the truth if I were you, Mr Longley.
3. I'd never forgive Raphaela if she lie __________________ to me.
4. If the suspect is not at home tomorrow, we have to ________________________ try again on Monday.

"So he didn't have a clue about anything?" Elvira asked, and took a sip of tonic. "The murder, the investigation, the..."

"Not the slightest idea," Hudson replied. "Or at least that's the impression he gave us. He could have been **performing**, mind you."

"I'm still not sure that Longley would kill Green just because he saw him arguing with his wife and possibly hitting her," Elvira said. "Even if Green did witness an attack, there's no evidence to suggest he knew about any regular violence."

"Which leads me to another important point," Hudson said. "George Ratcliffe told me today that Schmitt was supposed to wear a pirate costume at the party, but he gave it to Green at the last minute. Apparently, Green had arrived without a costume. Although Longley claims not to know either Schmitt or

to perform	*hier*: schauspielern

Green, maybe he did, in fact, know Schmitt. Maybe he knew that Aga had **confided in him**, and even suspected that they were having an affair. Look at it this way. If Longley knew Schmitt was going to be dressed as a pirate... **hey presto**, he's a target."

to confide in sb.	jmd. etw. anvertrauen
⚡ Hey presto!	Schwupps!
death trap	Todesfalle
leak	Leck
to counter sth.	einer Sache widersprechen
testimony	Zeugenaussage

Elvira looked confused. "An affair?" she asked.

"When Schmitt saw the pair arguing in the street, he heard Longley call Agnieszka a slut. So maybe he got the wrong man the first time, and tried again, turning Schmitt's car into a **death trap**."

"I'm still convinced Ewan O'Brian and Charlie Collins played a role," Elvira said slowly. "The full reports on the Chrimarsan flood make for interesting reading.(i) There was plenty of evi-dence to suggest it wasn't an accident: the pipes were only six months old. It was calculated that the **leak** occurred on a Friday evening, and the flood wasn't discovered until the following Monday morning. This allowed maximum time for damage."

She took another sip and then continued, "But one thing **countered** all of this evidence: Ewan O'Brian's **testimony**. He claimed to have invited Green to his house for drinks on Friday. How convenient that there were no CCTV cameras in Mr O'Brian's street to disprove this! The whole situation supports my theory that Green was a dangerous addition to the relationship between Collins and O'Brian. He must have been a source of pain, jealousy and constant fear. The easiest thing to do was to kill him."

> **To make for... reading** bedeutet „ist ... zu lesen". Das Phrasal Verb **to make for sth.** meint „etw. sein/ergeben".

Übung 55: Correct the mistakes. Lesen Sie weiter und korrigieren Sie die sechs Fehler im folgenden Absatz!

"It's possible," Hudson said, nodding its head as he spoke. "And I can see a possible connection to Schmitt's crash, too. Green said anything odd to Schmitt shortly after he was killed. He said they needed to talk 'man too man'. It seems he wants to tell him a secret. Maybe, in his drunken state, he wanted to tell Thomas about the fraude."

1. ________________ 4. ________________

2. ________________ 5. ________________

3. ________________ 6. ________________

"And maybe, in his paranoia, Ewan believed that Green had already confessed to Thomas, his new best friend," Elvira added. "In this case, Thomas was a threat, too."

Hudson nodded again.

Elvira took another sip of her tonic and then sat silently in thought for a few seconds.

"What is it?" Hudson asked.

"I was going to ask... No, it doesn't matter."

"Oh come on!" Hudson protested. "You can't start off like that and then not finish."

"Okay, then... I was wondering how the whole thing had

threat	Bedrohung

affected your relationship with Raphaela. I mean, on a personal level," she said.

Hudson sighed. Any kind of answer would be complicated, so he simply shared his confused thoughts with his colleague and friend.

faintest idea	leiseste Ahnung
to blush	erröten

"In all honesty, Elvira, I don't know where we stand at the moment. I mean, everything is still unclear. I don't know if Raphaela's talking to me or not. I don't know if she trusts me. And I haven't got the faintest idea what the future holds."

"I'm sorry," Elvira said with a sympathetic smile. "I know how much you like her."

Hudson blushed. He wasn't used to dealing with his emotions so publicly.

"There's one good thing, though," he said, trying to lift the mood. "If my theory is correct – if Thomas Schmitt was the target from the start – then Raphaela is safe. She didn't know Schmitt, so she'd have no reason to kill him. Besides, she knew he was dressed as a jester, not a pirate."

Relativsätze
Ist der Hauptsatz auch ohne den Relativsatz verständlich (**nicht notwendiger Relativsatz**), muss dieser - wie hier - durch Komma vom Hauptsatz abgehoben werden. Ein **notwendiger Relativsatz** wird nicht durch Komma vom Hauptsatz getrennt.

Elvira nodded her head as Hudson spoke, and then finished her glass of tonic.

"Another drink?" she asked.

"Just a second," Hudson replied, reaching for his phone, which was ringing in his pocket. (i)

"Forensics...," Hudson said when he looked at the screen.

Übung 56: Probability. Ergänzen Sie die fehlenden Wörter!

likely   possible   impossible   unlikely

1. Longley can't have known nothing about the murder - that's ________.
2. Schmitt was very scared, so it's ________ he slept well.
3. I don't think Trevor was responsible, but it's still ________.
4. Hudson is an experienced detective, so it is ________ ________ he will eventually identify the killer.

At the hospital the man had everything he needed. Syringe full of poison: check. Gag: check. Plan to get rid of Thomas Schmitt once and for all: check.

And he was wearing a disguise, too. It had been easy to steal a male nurse's uniform from a wash trolley. How brilliantly ironic, he thought to himself, that Thomas Schmitt loves fancy dress so much, and a costume is now playing a role in his murder.

He had everything planned. He would wait until the nurses had finished their evening checks before entering the ward. Then he would make his way to Schmitt's room. If anybody

syringe	Spritze
ϟ check	stimmt, abgehakt
gag	*hier*: Knebel
wash trolley	Wäschewagen
ward	(Krankenhaus-) Station

questioned him, he would say he was new and had lost his way in the huge building.

He was looking forward to seeing Schmitt suffer. Suffer, as he had suffered himself. Nobody understood his point of view, he thought. For a long time he had felt stressed, full of anger and self-doubt. But that had passed now, and none of that mattered. Who needs people's understanding when you have the power to play God?

Übung 57: Word reversal. Finden Sie die beschriebenen Begriffe und suchen Sie dann im obigen Abschnitt die rückwärts geschrieben Entsprechungen!

Beispiel: A cutting tool. saw – was

1. The opposite of 'lost' (e.g. a game) ____________
2. Use a pencil to create a picture ____________
3. Another words for 'puddings' ____________
4. A popular four-legged pet ____________

"I'm listening," Hudson said once the forensic scientist had introduced himself.

"The reason I'm calling so late is because we can confirm several important matters. First, someone did interfere with Mr Schmitt's car. There was a small hole in each of the rubber brake pipes. This was certainly no accident. Second, we've identified the hair found on the knife, and the fingerprints found on the

to interfere with	*hier*: sich zu schaffen machen an

car bonnet. They both led us to the same man: a certain Peter Shaw."

"Shaw?" Hudson asked, surprised.

"Yes. Mr Shaw was found guilty of **grievous bodily harm** four years ago. His prints and DNA were taken and kept on record."

"Can you provide me with an address?"

"12 Walton Street, Oxford."

There was no time to **delay**. He ended the call and immediately rang Sergeant Clayton.

"Peter Shaw?" Clayton asked. "Peter... Pete... Didn't Deborah Mitchell refer to her ex-boyfriend as Pete?"

"Possibly," Hudson replied. "I'll call her to find out and ring you back straight away. Get ready to leave, Sergeant!"

Deborah Mitchell answered the phone after a single ring.

grievous bodily harm	schwere Körperverletzung
to delay	verzögern
pleasantries *pl*	Höflichkeiten

Übung 58: Verb forms. Lesen Sie weiter und unterstreichen Sie die richtige Variante!

"Deborah, can you please tell us the name of your ex-boyfriend?" Hudson **1.** said / was saying, not wasting time with **pleasantries**. "The one you've **2.** been arguing / argued with a lot recently?"

"Pete," she said. "Pete Shaw. **3.** It's / It's being strange you should ask, Inspector. I've **4.** been visiting / been visited Thomas, but they've **5.** been closing / closed the ward for visitors now."

"I'm in the hospital car park now, heading back to my car," she continued. "Anyway, Pete's car is here, too. It's parked just a few cars from my own. It's an old yellow thing; it's definitely his."
Immediately, alarm bells started ringing in Hudson's head. Everything made sense now! Peter Shaw had killed Green in error. The jealous ex-boyfriend had murdered the pirate – but got the wrong man. So he then pierced the brake lines in Schmitt's car – but yet again, Schmitt had escaped death. So now he was at the hospital... making a third attempt on Schmitt's life?!
"Deborah, listen very carefully!" Hudson said in a calm yet urgent voice. "We have reason to believe that Peter Shaw is responsible for the murder of Alexander Green and the attempted murder of Thomas, too. You have to raise the alarm at the hospital NOW!"

Thomas Schmitt was feeling very sleepy when the nurse walked into his private room and closed the door behind him.
"Good evening, Mr Schmitt," the nurse said. "I've got your final injection for the day. It'll help you sleep."
Thomas found the nurse strangely familiar. Had they met before? Or had he seen him in photographs? He was too tired to think about it now.
"Thanks, but the other nurse gave me something to help me sleep. I don't think I need anything else," he said with a yawn.
"I've got something which will help you sleep much deeper, though," the nurse said. "Here, see."
A syringe full of a clear liquid appeared before Thomas's eyes.

to pierce	durchstechen
attempt on sb.'s life	Mordanschlag, Attentat
yawn	Gähnen

to clench one's fist	die Hand zur Faust ballen
prick	Stich
fluid	Flüssigkeit
unease	Unbehagen

The nurse was holding it up for him to see.

"Come on, Mr Schmitt. It's doctor's orders," the nurse said in a friendly voice. "Clench your fist, please. It's just a short, sharp prick, then it'll all be over."

Thomas yawned again. Moonlight was shining brightly through the window, creating an odd, dreamlike atmosphere.

Usually Elvira Elliot drove much too quickly for Hudson's liking, but now she could not drive quickly enough. The roads were clear, and the hospital was less than two miles from the hotel. Nevertheless, the journey seemed to take forever.

Sergeant Clayton and several police cars were on their way to the hospital, too. The sooner an officer was at Schmitt's bedside, the safer he was. But with the hospital so close to the George Hotel, Hudson doubted they would get there any quicker than Elvira in her lightning-fast sports car. Hudson was counting the seconds as they sped down the streets. He was in no doubt now that Thomas Schmitt was in very real danger.

"No," Thomas Schmitt said to the nurse.

"Sorry, Mr Schmitt? Don't you understand? You need this injection to get a good night's sleep."

Something wasn't right, thought Thomas. The nurse was acting oddly, and he was far too eager to inject the fluid into his arm. What was worse, Thomas could see the nurse's unease every time a sound came from the corridor.

"Come on now, Mr Schmitt. I've got a lot more patients to see this evening. I can't wait here with you all night."

cloth	Tuch
to dodge death	dem Tod ausweichen

Thomas reached out to press the button at the side of his bed to call a nurse, but the man quickly pulled the button out of his reach. Then he suddenly pulled a piece of cloth from his pocket.

"You've dodged death twice," the man said, trying to stay calm. "I refuse to let you do so a third time. If it wasn't for you, Debbie would still be with me!"

Übung 59: Questions to the text. Beantworten Sie die folgenden Fragen zum Text!

1. Was Thomas sharing a room with other patients?

   ____

2. What did the nurse ask Thomas to do so that he could give him the injection?

   ____

3. How was Hudson's attitude to Elvira's driving different to usual?

   ____

4. How sure was Hudson that Thomas was in danger?

   ____

Thomas could see what was happening, but he was tired and his reactions were slow. Before he could scream, the man had tied the gag around his mouth.

In panic, Thomas tried to struggle, but the man was too strong. He had **pinned** Thomas to the bed with his left arm, and the needle in his right hand was moving closer and closer to Thomas's left arm.

to pin sb.	jmd. nieder-drücken
to usher out	hinausführen
ϟ God-knows-what	was auch immer

Suddenly, the door swung open and Thomas heard a woman scream in panic.

"Pete!" Debbie Mitchell cried. "What the hell's going on?"

Two security guards were standing behind her. One of them reached out and flicked the light switch.

"Don't come any closer!" Peter Shaw cried, and swung the needle towards Debbie. "Stay away from me!"

"Put the needle down!" one of security guards cried, taking a step forward.

The other guard **ushered** Debbie **out** of the room, but she was shouting and struggling, fully aware of how close the needle was to her boyfriend's arm.

Oh my God, Debbie's at the centre of all this! Thomas thought in shock. Pete tried to kill me to get her back. And now he's waving a syringe full of **God-knows-what** around the room!

The situation seemed absurd. And yet, absurd as it was, the unfolding scenario was real and very frightening.

"Put the needle down, Pete!" Debbie cried, fighting the security guard to get back into the room.

"Stay back!" the guard ordered Debbie. "Stay out of the room!"

"This isn't worth...," Debbie cried.

"Don't tell me what it's worth!" Pete cried in passionate anger. "When you left me, I lost everything I had. So I've got nothing to lose, right? You're all I want, Debbie! I've talked and I've talked and I've talked, and still you won't listen. If this is what it takes to get you back, then this is what I'm prepared to do."

"You still don't understand, do you?" Debbie said, her voice trembling.

The security guard was now holding her firmly. They were a safe distance from the madman armed with a syringe.

"I'm *never* going to take you back," Debbie screamed. "Never!"

Pete then moved the needle back, aiming it directly towards Thomas's arm.

Thomas was turning left and right, but he was too weak to get away. Pete was still holding him tight.

to inch towards	(sich) ganz langsam zubewegen auf

Übung 60: Missing body parts! Lesen Sie weiter und ergänzen Sie die fehlenden Körperteile!

eye | brain | hand | arm | vein

Thomas could almost see Pete's **1.** ______ ticking as he considered his next move. The **2.** ______ holding the needle was beginning to shake. He **inched** it **towards** the largest visible **3.** ______ in Thomas's **4.** ______.

"Put the needle down!" the nearest security guard shouted again, but still kept back.

After a long, dangerous silence, Pete turned and looked Debbie in the **5.** ______.

"Never?" he asked.

The man looked as if he was about the burst into tears.

"Never," Debbie answered without a trace of doubt.

Pete raised the syringe and lined it up with his own heart.

to line sth. up with	etw. ausrichten auf
to observe	beobachten
petrified	wie versteinert
handcuffs	Handschellen
to escort	geleiten

"Put the weapon down!" Sergeant Clayton shouted as he burst into the room, taking the whole group by surprise.

He was aiming a gun at Shaw.

"Place the weapon on the ground and put your hands in the air!"

Hudson stepped into the room behind Clayton and observed the scene.

Shaw's whole body was physically shaking; he was petrified by the situation he had created. He was wearing a nurse's uniform that was far too big for a short man like himself. He had dark rings around his eyes, and sweat was dripping down his forehead.

"Put the weapon on the floor!" Clayton shouted again, just as aggressively as the first time.

Slowly, Shaw knelt to the ground and placed the needle on the floor. Without a second's delay, Clayton grabbed Shaw's arms. With Hudson's help, he pulled the man's arms around his back and secured him in handcuffs.

"Well," Hudson said to Shaw, "you've certainly been providing me and my colleagues with fun and games for the past couple of days. I can't wait to hear your story, Mr Shaw."

"It was all for you!" Shaw cried to Debbie, ignoring Hudson.

"Peter Shaw," Clayton said, "I'm arresting you on suspicion of murder and attempted murder."

The two security guards helped Hudson and Clayton to escort

Shaw out of the room. At the same time, two doctors rushed to Thomas Schmitt's bedside, asking what Shaw had done.

"Nothing, I'm fine," Thomas replied. "Debbie arrived just in time."

"Thomas!" Debbie cried, running back into the room. "Thomas, thank God you're..."

Debbie's words became incomprehensible as the young woman burst into tears. She threw her arms across her boyfriend's chest and sobbed her heart out.

Übung 61: Translation. Übersetzen Sie die folgenden Sätze ins Englische!

1. Der Polizist richtete die Pistole auf den Jungen.

   ____

2. Die Polizei nahm den Arzt unverzüglich fest.

   ____

3. Das Mädchen stürzte in das Zimmer hinein.

   ____

4. Der Wachmann war wie versteinert.

   ____

Two police cars were just arriving when Hudson and Clayton reached the exit. Shaw was in handcuffs and unable to escape their grip; it was perfect timing to take him away to the station. Elvira had been waiting outside, ready to direct the police to Schmitt's ward. Now, back in her car and following the police

grip	Griff
↯ juicy	*hier*: interessant, reizvoll

cars out of the car park, she was not happy to have missed out on the action.
"We insurance investigators always miss the juicy bits," she said to Hudson, her passenger. "Maybe I need a change of career."
"Not so fast, Elvira," Hudson replied with a smile. "We may have got Shaw, but there are still a few pieces that need putting together. Fraud? Domestic violence? I was counting on your help."
"Fraud and domestic violence?" Elvira asked, thinking as she said each word. "Go on then, James. I'm in."
And with that she pulled out of the car park, put her foot on the accelerator and sped off down the road.

Abschlusstest

Übung 1: Definitions. Welches Wort ist gemeint?

1. The police department which analyzes scientific evidence.

2. Violent behaviour towards members of the same household.

3. To injure someone with a sharp, pointed object.

4. The politically correct term for 'American Indians'.

Übung 2: Multiple choice. Kreuzen Sie die richtige Antwort an!

1. On Rose Monday, how long had Thomas Schmitt been working in Britain?
   - a) ❐ three months
   - b) ❐ five months

2. What does Raphaela do at Oxford University?

a) ❒ She is a lecturer.

b) ❒ She is a student of neuroscience.

3. Where are the headquarters of Thames Valley Police located?

a) ❒ Cowley

b) ❒ Kidlington

4. Where does George Ratcliffe come from?

a) ❒ Newcastle

b) ❒ London

Übung 3: Translation quiz. Übersetzen Sie und enträtseln Sie das Lösungswort!

1. Narr ☐ _ _ _ _ _
2. Lagerhaus _ _ _ ☐ _ _ _ _ _
3. Absolvent _ _ ☐ _ _ _ _ _
4. slavisch _ ☐ _ _ _ _
5. Stiefel _ _ ☐ _
6. unbeliebt ☐ _ _ _ _ _ _ _ _
7. sauer ☐ _ _ _
8. Augenklappe _ ☐ _ _ _ _ _ _

Lösung: ☐ ☐ ☐ ☐ ☐ ☐ ☐ ☐

Übung 4: Fill in the blanks. Ergänzen Sie die fehlenden Bestimmungswörter!

both   either   neither   neither

1. "I'm not impressed," the woman remarked. "I must say, ________ of the dishes look very tasty."
2. I'm not bothered. I'll take ________.
3. I love them so much I'll take ________.
4. During the interview, ________ Longley nor his girlfriend were very helpful.

Übung 5: Who said that? Erinnern Sie sich daran, wer das gesagt hat? Ordnen Sie zu!

1. ☐ "Whatever I wear, it will definitely be fabulous."
2. ☐ "A sexist, pig-headed pervert for a boss."
3. ☐ "It was his birthday. He should have been the pirate. End of story."
4. ☐ "If I wanted the opinion of a schoolgirl, I'd ask for it."

a) Ewan O'Brian

b) George Ratcliffe

c) Angela Haffner

d) Alexander Green

Übung 6: Idiomatic expressions. Ergänzen Sie die Ausdrücke und übersetzen Sie sie!

1. Worse things happen at ________.

   ____

2. A ________ for your thoughts.

   ____

3. To walk on thin ________.

   ____

4. To prick up one's ________.

   ____

5. Don't get your ________ in a twist.

   ____

Übung 7: Word search. Finden Sie die sieben Gebäude, in denen die Handlung der Geschichte stattgefunden hat!

G	A	A	V	I	M	O	R	T	U	A	R	Y
T	W	A	R	E	H	O	U	S	E	O	E	E
A	G	I	P	C	V	Q	H	N	A	F	I	P
S	S	F	A	E	E	Z	O	U	W	F	I	K
P	O	L	I	C	E	S	T	A	T	I	O	N
T	O	A	S	D	B	I	E	J	U	C	R	E
A	P	T	X	C	K	E	L	S	L	E	I	D
H	O	U	S	E	N	M	A	E	J	P	L	L

Lösungen

Übung 1: **1.** d **2.** a **3.** c **4.** b

Übung 2: **1.** isn't it **2.** aren't you **3.** won't it **4.** haven't I

Übung 3: **1.** like **2.** may **3.** Make **4.** have

Übung 4: **1.** u (you) **2.** 1 (one) **3.** 2 (too) **4.** C (see)

Übung 5: **1.** richtig **2.** richtig **3.** falsch (When Alexander was in Ewan's office, Thomas was talking to George.) **4.** falsch (Thomas was lying when he said that he had to finish his presentation.)

Übung 6: **1.** to **2.** after **3.** of **4.** on **5.** – **6.** of

Übung 7:

1 T	2 E	3 A	4 R	5 S	6 T
20 E	21 A	22 N	23 E	24 R	7 O
19 L	32 R	33 L	34 I	25 E	8 M
18 C	31 A	36 G	35 N	26 S	9 A
17 I	30 D	29 N	28 O	27 P	10 C
16 R	15 O	14 T	13 S	12 I	11 H

Übung 8: **1.** I'm going to introduce **2.** still **3.** everyone **4.** week

Übung 9: **1.** beer **2.** wardrobe **3.** forget **4.** impressed

Übung 10:

1	2	3	4	5
d	e	c	b	a

Übung 11: **1.** promise **2.** costume **3.** camper **4.** dress **5.** finger-nails **6.** curly

Übung 12: **1.** Call me back! **2.** Turn the music down! / Turn down the music! **3.** Leave a message after the tone! **4.** Get here as quickly as you can!

Übung 13: **1.** drunk **2.** calm **3.** sober **4.** unconvincing **5.** fun

Übung 14: **1.** b **2.** d **3.** a **4.** c

Übung 15: **1.** ran **2.** cried **3.** continued **4.** searched **5.** put **6.** were

Übung 16: **1.** street lamp **2.** still **3.** fear **4.** engine **5.** polite **6.** pocket **7.** swear **8.** waistcoat
Lösung: lifeless

Übung 17: **1.** pretend **2.** neighbour **3.** ambulance **4.** extremely

Übung 18: **1.** b **2.** b **3.** a **4.** a

Übung 19: **1.** help **2.** days **3.** job **4.** Headquarters

Übung 20: **1.** Hudson was greeted by Sir Fleming at the police station. **2.** Alex Green's body was found by Thomas. **3.** The party is being hosted by two of my friends. **4.** Has the body been identified (by anyone)?

Übung 21: **1.** mobile phone **2.** Father Christmas **3.** driving licence **4.** to ring sb. **5.** holiday

Übung 22: **1.** It's sickening **2.** quite **3.** enemies **4.** To **5.** an understatement **6.** Some of my colleagues

Übung 23:

S	U	G	G	E	S	T	U	S	B
S	A	T	Y	V	P	H	U	H	C
Q	C	V	Y	B	E	Z	H	O	X
T	E	N	I	E	A	R	G	U	E
E	S	P	R	A	K	T	H	T	R
L	P	I	E	E	P	M	J	A	K
L	E	A	S	K	A	P	E	N	N
O	A	L	L	R	U	C	A	L	L

Übung 24: **1.** phone **2.** girlfriend **3.** face **4.** room **5.** question

Übung 25: **1.** obvious **2.** to request **3.** to check **4.** state-of the-art

Übung 26: **1.** suspicious **2.** absolute **3.** simply **4.** completely **5.** whole **6.** extremely **7.** wrong

Übung 27: **1.** d **2.** b **3.** a **4.** c

Übung 28: **1.** interrupted **2.** want **3.** am telling **4.** be **5.** isn't **6.** found

Übung 29: **1.** falsch (Mallika Soni looked nothing like the other pathologists Hudson had worked with.) **2.** richtig **3.** falsch (Hudson still needed an officer to check if a knife was missing.) **4.** falsch (She said they would have to wait for the test results.)

Übung 30:

			1 M	Y	S	T	E	2 R	Y	
								E		
3 T								T		
4 H	O	S	P	I	5 T	A	L	I	Z	E
U					I			R		
G			6 S	A	M	P	L	E		
					I					
	7 W	O	U	N	D					

Übung 31: **1.** in **2.** behind **3.** from **4.** out **5.** After

Übung 32: **1.** d **2.** a **3.** b **4.** c

Übung 33: **1.** anything **2.** everything **3.** something **4.** anything

Übung 34: **1.** true **2.** suspicion **3.** station **4.** interview

Übung 35: **1.** bloke **2.** pretty **3.** to piss someone off **4.** Get lost! **5.** racket

Übung 36: **1.** soap opera **2.** obvious **3.** stairway **4.** backyard **5.** valuable **6.** present **7.** convincing **8.** annoyed
Lösung: evidence

Übung 37: **1.** He wants advice on how to tell Sergeant Clayton and Sir Fleming about his relationship with Raphaela. **2.** He suggests they meet at the bar in the George Hotel. **3.** His title is Chief Inspector (of Thames Valley Police). **4.** He plans to interview the employees of Chrimarsan Sauerkraut.

Übung 38: **1.** b **2.** d **3.** c **4.** a

Übung 39: **1.** Don't **2.** make **3.** made **4.** doesn't

Übung 40: **1.** appear **2.** lifeless **3.** wide awake **4.** main road **5.** in a foul mood

Übung 41: **1.** a **2.** d **3.** c **4.** b

Übung 42: **1.** time **2.** midnight **3.** track **4.** hard **5.** way

Übung 43: **1.** while **2.** once **3.** until **4.** since

Übung 44:

1 P	2 A	3 R	4 T	5 N	6 E	7 R
22 I	23 C	24 H	25 E	26 S	27 T	8 A
21 T	36 E	37 M	38 O	39 T	28 A	9 P
20 E	35 M	42 N	41 O	40 I	29 C	10 H
19 G	34 I	33 R	32 C	31 I	30 T	11 A
18 O	17 L	16 O	15 P	14 A	13 L	12 E

Übung 45: **1.** ring **2.** second **3.** unknown **4.** voice **5.** girlfriend

Übung 46: **1.** b **2.** c **3.** a **4.** d

Übung 47: **1.** timing **2.** finally **3.** convenient **4.** murder **5.** party

Übung 48: **1.** Hudson fand den Gedanken nicht sehr verlockend, Sir Fleming von Raphaela zu erzählen. **2.** Ich habe mir ein Bein gebrochen und es musste gegipst werden! **3.** Ich kann keine Anrufe machen, weil mein Handy defekt ist. **4.** Ich bin überhaupt nicht abergläubisch.

Übung 49: **1.** more rational, most rational **2.** heavier, heaviest **3.** fitter, fittest **4.** better, best

Übung 50: **1.** picked **2.** was **3.** know **4.** Let **5.** don't consider **6.** wanted **7.** to give **8.** was **9.** replied

Übung 51:

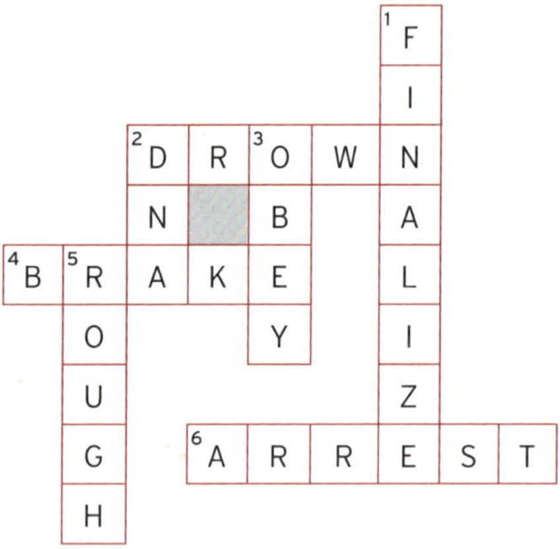

Übung 52: **1.** military **2.** birthday **3.** costume **4.** bothered **5.** day **6.** salary

Übung 53: **1.** He was eating a chocolate bar. **2.** George's later memories of the party are cloudy. **3.** George described her as "a hot bit of stuff". **4.** Hudson thinks that the killer murdered Alexander Green by accident – the real target was Thomas Schmitt.

Übung 54: **1.** is **2.** would tell **3.** lied **4.** will have to

Übung 55: **1.** his head **2.** said something **3.** shortly before **4.** 'man to man' **5.** wanted **6.** fraud

Übung 56: **1.** impossible **2.** unlikely **3.** possible **4.** likely

Übung 57: **1.** won - now **2.** draw - ward **3.** desserts - stressed **4.** dog - God

Übung 58: **1.** said **2.** been arguing **3.** It's **4.** been visiting **5.** closed

Übung 59: **1.** No. He had a private room. **2.** The nurse asked Thomas to clench his fist. **3.** Usually Hudson finds Elvira drives too fast, but this time he was glad about it. **4.** Hudson was in no doubt/certain that Thomas was in danger.

Übung 60: **1.** brain **2.** hand **3.** vein **4.** arm **5.** eye

Übung 61: **1.** The policeman aimed the gun at the boy. **2.** The police arrested the doctor without delay. **3.** The girl burst into the room. **4.** The security guard was petrified.

Abschlusstest

Übung 1: **1.** forensics **2.** domestic violence **3.** stab **4.** Native American

Übung 2: **1.** b **2.** a **3.** b **4.** a

Übung 3: **1.** jester **2.** warehouse **3.** graduate **4.** Slavic **5.** boot **6.** unpopular **7.** sour **8.** eyepatch
Lösung: jealousy

Übung 4: **1.** neither **2.** either **3.** both **4.** neither

Übung 5: **1.** a **2.** c **3.** b **4.** d

Übung 6: **1.** sea - Es könnte schlimmer sein. **2.** penny - Was denkst du gerade? **3.** ice - sich auf dünnem Eis bewegen **4.** ears - die Ohren spitzen **5.** knickers - Bleib ruhig. / Reg dich nicht auf.

Übung 7:

G	A	A	V	I	M	O	R	T	U	A	R	Y
T	W	A	R	E	H	O	U	S	E	O	E	E
A	G	I	P	C	V	Q	H	N	A	F	I	P
S	S	F	A	E	E	Z	O	U	W	F	I	K
P	O	L	I	C	E	S	T	A	T	I	O	N
T	O	A	S	D	B	I	E	J	U	C	R	E
A	P	T	X	C	K	E	L	S	L	E	I	D
H	O	U	S	E	N	M	A	E	J	P	L	L

Glossar

↯ = umgangssprachlich

accelerate	Gas geben
account	Bericht
Accounts Manager	Leiter(in) der Buchhaltung
to admit	zugeben
alert	wachsam, auf der Hut
anxiety	Sorge
A penny for your thoughts.	Ich würde gerne wissen, was du denkst.
apologetic	entschuldigend
apparently	anscheinend
to appeal for witnesses	um Zeugenaussagen bitten
appealing	verlockend
astounding	erstaunlich
attempted murder	Mordversuch
attempt on sb.'s life	Mordanschlag, Attentat
↯ at the end of the day	letzten Endes
at the top of one's voice	aus vollem Hals
awful	furchtbar
awkward	*hier*: unangenehm
to be abused	misshandelt werden
bearded	bärtig
to be fast asleep	tief und fest schlafen
to be in the know	Bescheid wissen
to be mistaken	sich täuschen
bewildered	verwirrt
bin bag	Müllbeutel

black eye	blaues Auge
to blast out	dröhnen
ϟ bloke	Kerl
ϟ bloody kraut	verdammte(r) Deutsche(r)
bluntly	unverblümt
to blush	erröten
bombshell	Bombe
to bother	stören
branch	*hier*: Zweigstelle
breakdown	*hier*: Aufgliederung, Darstellung
brick	Ziegelstein
to bring (brought, brought) up	*hier*: zur Sprache bringen
bruising	Bluterguss
bully	Tyrann
bun	*hier*: Haarknoten
bunch	*hier*: Haufen
bunch of keys	Schlüsselbund
to burst (burst, burst)	platzen
to burst out laughing	in Gelächter ausbrechen
Business before pleasure.	Erst die Arbeit, dann das Vergnügen.
to buy a story	jmd. eine Geschichte abkaufen
calling card	Visitenkarte
camouflage	Tarnung
camp	affektiert, übertrieben
cardigan	Strickjacke
casual(ly)	locker
CCTV	Videoüberwachung
ϟ check	stimmt, abgehakt
checkout	Kasse
cheek	Wange
to choke	sich verschlucken
to choose to ignore sth.	etw. nicht hören wollen
to chuckle	kichern
to claim	behaupten
to clear sb.	*hier*: jmd. entlasten

to clench one's fist	die Hand zur Faust ballen
cloth	Tuch
clueless	ahnungslos
coincidence	Zufall
to come (came, come) forward	sich melden
complaint	Beschwerde
to confide in sb.	jmd. etw. anvertrauen
confirmation	Bestätigung
convenient	praktisch, passend
conviction	Überzeugung
convinced	überzeugt, sicher
to cope with	zurechtkommen mit
to cordon off	absperren
to counter sth.	einer Sache widersprechen
to crash	verunglücken
creepy	gruselig
to curse	fluchen
deafening	ohrenbetäubend
death trap	Todesfalle
to delay	verzögern
delivery	Lieferung
deputy	*hier*: Vize-
to devour	verschlingen
dim	schwach, trüb
discreet	diskret
disgusting	widerlich
to disprove	widerlegen
disrespectful	respektlos
to divert	umleiten
to dodge death	dem Tod ausweichen
ϟ Don't get your knickers in a twist.	Reg dich nicht auf.
ϟ drag	Fummel
drama graduate	ausgebildete(r) Schauspieler(in)
to draw conclusions	Schlüsse ziehen
to drown	ertrinken

dull	eintönig
to duly obey	ordnungsgemäß Folge leisten
eager	begierig
emotional blackmail	emotional unter Druck setzen
employee	Mitarbeiter(in)
encounter	Begegnung
⚡ End of story.	Basta!, Und Schluss.
escapade	*hier*: Abenteuer, Streich
to escort	geleiten
evidence	Beweismittel
exasperated	aufgebracht
to exceed	übertreffen
exception	Ausnahme
to exclaim	(aus)rufen
exhausting	anstrengend
eyepatch	Augenklappe
fabric	Stoff
to fade	verblassen
failure	*hier*: Reinfall
faintest idea	leiseste Ahnung
⚡ to fancy sth.	Lust auf etw. haben
fancy dress	Verkleidung
figure	Gestalt
to finalize	endgültig ausarbeiten
to flash	*hier*: aufleuchten
⚡ flavour of the month	die derzeitige Nummer eins
to flee (fled, fled)	flüchten
to flick a switch	einen Schalter umlegen
fluid	Flüssigkeit
forensics	Gerichtsmedizin
forward	*hier*: vorlaut
foul	mies, fürchterlich
foul play	falsches Spiel, Verbrechen
fraud	Betrug
gadget	technische Spielerei
gag	*hier*: Knebel
genuinely	echt

Geordie	Person aus Newcastle
to get back to sb.	sich wieder bei jmd. melden
ϟ Get lost!	Hau ab!
to get off scot-free	ungeschoren davonkommen
to get to the bottom of sth.	einer Sache auf den Grund gehen
giddy excitement	ausgelassene Freude
ginger-haired	rothaarig
to give one's all	alles geben
glance	Blick
glare	wütender Blick
ϟ God-knows-what	was auch immer
ϟ to go out with a bang	mit einem Bombenerfolg enden
to grab	greifen
grievous bodily harm	schwere Körperverletzung
grimly	grimmig
grip	Griff
to hail a taxi	ein Taxi heranwinken
handcuffs *pl*	Handschellen
to harass	belästigen
to have a love interest	in jmd. verliebt sein
to have a real brush with death	dem Tode knapp entronnen sein
head	*hier*: Chef(in), Leiter(in)
headdress	Kopfschmuck
to head straight to	direkt zugehen auf
sb.'s heart sank	jmd. wurde das Herz schwer
ϟ Hey presto!	Schwupps!
hint	Spur, Hauch
to hospitalize	*hier*: krankenhausreif schlagen
host	Gastgeber(in)
ϟ hot bit of stuff	scharfe Braut, heißes Gerät
I'm not missing out!	Ich lass mir das nicht entgehen!
to imply	andeuten
impressed	beeindruckt
in a fluster	aufgeregt
in an instant	augenblicklich, im Nu

to inch towards	(sich) ganz langsam zubewegen auf
incident	Vorfall
inconceivable	unvorstellbar
to indicate	*hier*: blinken
industrial estate	Industriepark
in exasperation	verärgert
insurance	Versicherung
intense	*hier*: leidenschaftlich
to interfere with	*hier*: sich zu schaffen machen an
intern	Praktikant(in)
to interrogate	verhören
intimacy	Vertrautheit
to investigate	untersuchen
IT	Informationstechnik
sb.'s jaw dropped	jmd. fiel die Kinnlade herunter
jester	(Hof-)Narr
to jot down	(schnell) notieren
judgement	*hier*: Urteilsfähigkeit
ϟ juicy	*hier*: interessant, reizvoll
to jump in shock	vor Schreck zusammenzucken
key	*hier*: zentral, entscheidend
to kneel (knelt, knelt) down	sich hinknien
leak	Leck
to leave one's mark	seine Spuren hinterlassen
lecturer in neuroscience	Dozent(in) der Neurowissenschaften
Let's get down to business.	Kommen wir zur Sache.
to line sth. up with	etw. ausrichten auf
lonely hearts section	Kontaktanzeigen
to lust after sb.	jmd. begehren
to make (made, made) it	es schaffen
to make sb.'s life a misery	jmd. das Leben zur Hölle machen
to mask	verbergen
ϟ mate	Kumpel
to mingle with the guests	sich unter die Gäste mischen

miracle	Wunder
misconduct	Fehlverhalten
miserable	elend
to mistake sb. for sb. else	jmd. verwechseln
modest	zurückhaltend
mortuary	Leichenhalle
mugging	Straßenraub
to mutter	murmeln
mutual enemy	gemeinsamer Feind
native	Einheimische(r)
nervous wreck	Nervenbündel
new ground	Neuland
nonchalantly	gleichgültig
nosy	neugierig
not-so-delightful	nicht gerade reizend
objective	Ziel
to observe	beobachten
obvious(ly)	offensichtlich
odd(ly)	merkwürdig
offended	beleidigt
ϟ Oi!	He!
out-of-character	ungewöhnlich
over-active imagination	lebhafte Fantasie
to overhear (-heard, -heard)	zufällig mithören
over-protective	überfürsorglich
overwhelmed	überwältigt
to owe	schulden
packaging	Verpackung(en)
pale	blass
pane	(Fenster-)Scheibe
paramedic	Rettungssanitäter(in)
partner in crime	Komplize/Komplizin
passageway	Durchgang
patio	Veranda
patronizing	gönnerhaft
peculiar	seltsam
pensively	nachdenklich

to perform	*hier*: schauspielern
performance	*hier*: Leistung
personal ties *pl*	persönliche Bande
to persuade	überzeugen
pervert	Perverse(r)
petrified	wie versteinert
to pierce	durchstechen
pigtails *pl*	Zöpfe
to pin sb.	jmd. niederdrücken
pinstripe suit	Nadelstreifenanzug
pipe	Rohr
plain(ly)	schlicht
plaster	Gips
pleasantries *pl*	Höflichkeiten
plump	mollig
to praise	loben
to pretend	vorgeben
prick	Stich
to prick up one's ears	die Ohren spitzen
prime suspect	Hauptverdächtige(r)
prime target	klare Zielscheibe
production plant	Fertigungsanlage
proper officer	waschechter Offizier
to provide	bereitstellen
to pursue	verfolgen
pushchair	Kinderwagen
puzzled	verblüfft, verwirrt
ϟ racket	Krach
to range from ... to	reichen von ... bis
redundancy payout	Abfindung
to rely on sb.	sich auf jmd. verlassen
reminder	Erinnerung
to rephrase	neu formulieren
resentment	Verbitterung
to retire	in Rente gehen
to reveal	enthüllen
ripped	aufgerissen

rock	Stein
salary	Gehalt
sales pitch	Angebot (Vertrieb)
sample	Probe
screech	Quietschen
self-assured	selbstsicher
semi-detached	Doppelhaushälfte
sensitive	sensibel
to set (set, set) off	losfahren
severely	heftig
to shake (shook, shaken)	*hier*: zittern
short-staffed	knapp an Personal
to sigh	seufzen
to skid	schlittern
to slide	*hier*: schieben
slightly	ein wenig
slur	Lallen
ϟ slut	Schlampe
to snap	*hier*: blaffen
sob	Schluchzen
sober	nüchtern
softly	*hier*: leise
ϟ to sort things out	eine Sache in Ordnung bringen
spacious	weitläufig
to speculate	vermuten
to speed (sped, sped) off	davonbrausen
split personality	gespaltene Persönlichkeit
split second	Sekundenbruchteil
to spoil	verderben
to stab	stechen
stab wound	Stichwunde
to stagger	schwanken
to stand on the sidelines	unbeteiligter Zuschauer sein
state-of-the-art	hochmodern
steep	steil
strand	Strähne
to strut	stolzieren

to suggest sth.	*hier*: hindeuten auf
to suit sb.	jmd. stehen
superstitious	abergläubisch
superstore	großer Supermarkt
suspect	Verdächtige(r)
to suspend sth.	etw. aufhängen
swearing	Fluchen
syringe	Spritze
to tamper with	sich zu schaffen machen an
to target sb.	jmd. ins Visier nehmen
tension	Spannung
terraced house	Reihenhaus
terrified	total verängstigt
testimony	Zeugenaussage
text message	SMS
the latter	letzteres
The line had gone dead.	Die Leitung war tot.
the more..., the more...	je mehr ..., desto mehr ...
The plot seems so thick.	Der Fall scheint so komplex.
to think straight	klar denken
threat	Bedrohung
to throttle sb.	jmd. erdrosseln
thug	Schläger(typ)
to tick off	abhaken
to tie in with sth.	in Verbindung stehen mit
timid	ängstlich
to torture	quälen, foltern
tracksuit bottoms	Jogginghose
trapped	gefangen
treat	Leckerei
trustworthy	vertrauenswürdig
tyre	Reifen
unappreciated	nicht gewürdigt
uncomfortable	*hier*: unbehaglich
unconscious	bewusstlos
under one's breath	leise vor sich hin
unease	Unbehagen

unfaithful	untreu
to unfold	sich entwickeln
unmistakable	unverkennbar
to usher out	hinausführen
vague	vage, ausweichend
valuable	wertvoll
to vandalize	mutwillig beschädigen
victim	Opfer
violently	*hier*: heftig
vital	entscheidend
waistcoat	Weste
ward	(Krankenhaus-)Station
warehouse	Lagerhaus
wash trolley	Wäschewagen
We go back a long way.	Wir kennen uns schon ewig.
wig	Perücke
wink	Zwinkern
to wipe	wischen
with all due respect	bei allem nötigen Respekt
to withhold information	Informationen unterschlagen
wizard	Zauberer
Worse things happen at sea.	Es könnte schlimmer sein.
to worship	verehren
wreckage	Wrack(teile)
wrist	Handgelenk
yawn	Gähnen
4x4 (four-by-four)	Allradfahrzeug

Verzeichnis der Übungen

Abschlusstest

Lernkrimi Lektüren Englisch

A1

A Cry in the Darkness
Kurzkrimis
ISBN 978-3-8174-1974-6

Deadly Thanksgiving
Kurzkrimis
ISBN 978-3-8174-1756-8

Death at Land's End
Kurzkrimis
ISBN 978-3-8174-9658-7

The Murderer Next Door
Kurzkrimis
ISBN 978-3-8174-1952-4

A2

Blood and Breakfast
Kurzkrimis
ISBN 978-3-8174-1385-0

Deadly Business
Kurzkrimis
ISBN 978-3-8174-1969-2

Last Exit Waterloo Bridge
Kurzkrimis
ISBN 978-3-8174-1863-3

Murder at Teatime
Kurzkrimis
ISBN 978-3-8174-1856-5

Learning by Killing
Kurzkrimis
ISBN 978-3-8174-1388-1

Long Time No Kill
Classic
ISBN 978-3-8174-9794-2

B1

Belfast Secrets
Kurzkrimis
ISBN 978-3-8174-1955-5

Death Comes Knocking
Kurzkrimis
ISBN 978-3-8174-7945-0

Murderous Network
Kurzkrimis
ISBN 978-3-8174-1956-2

Art and Ashes
Classic
ISBN 978-3-8174-9493-4

Cook and Kill
Classic
ISBN 978-3-8174-9492-7

Deadly Mistake
Classic
ISBN 978-3-8174-1954-8

Death Wasn't the Deal
Classic
ISBN 978-3-8174-9491-0

Murderous Collection
Sammelband
ISBN 978-3-8174-1872-5

Murder Inside
Sammelband
ISBN 978-3-8174-1914-2

Bone by Bone
Lernthriller
ISBN 978-3-8174-9497-2

Faceless Killer
Lernthriller
ISBN 978-3-8174-1982-1

Massacre United
Lernthriller
ISBN 978-3-8174-9319-7

Lernkrimi Lektüren Englisch

B2

Bloody Diamonds
Classic
ISBN 978-3-8174-9494-1

London Is Killing Me
Classic
ISBN 978-3-8174-1910-4

Nobody Dies Twice
Classic
ISBN 978-3-8174-9495-8

Did I Kill Him?
Thriller
ISBN 978-3-8174-1958-6

C1

A Scottish Murder Mystery
Classic
ISBN 978-3-8174-1977-7

Keep Calm and Carry On Killing
Classic
ISBN 978-3-8174-1980-7

Lernkrimi Comic Englisch

A1

Chasing Bloody Mary
ISBN 978-3-8174-1655-4

Lernkrimi Sprachkurs Englisch

A1/A2

Lernkrimi Sprachkurs
ISBN 978-3-8174-7844-5

Lernkrimi Hörbücher Englisch

A1

Black Wedding
ISBN 978-3-8174-1817-6

Dangerous Deals
ISBN 978-3-8174-1989-3

A2

A Shot in the Night
ISBN 978-3-8174-8202-3

The Butterworth Mystery
ISBN 978-3-8174-8203-0

Death Wish
ISBN 978-3-8174-1959-3

Strangled
ISBN 978-3-8174-1876-3

B1

Bloody Revenge
ISBN 978-3-8174-8860-5

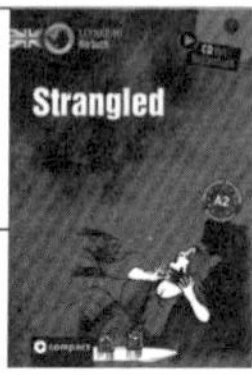

B2

Bloody Legacy
ISBN 978-3-8174-7676-3

Crime & Company
ISBN 978-3-8174-8976-3

Murder at the Office
ISBN 978-3-8174-7747-0

Lernkrimi Rätselblöcke Englisch

A1

Murderous Games
ISBN 978-3-8174-1960-9

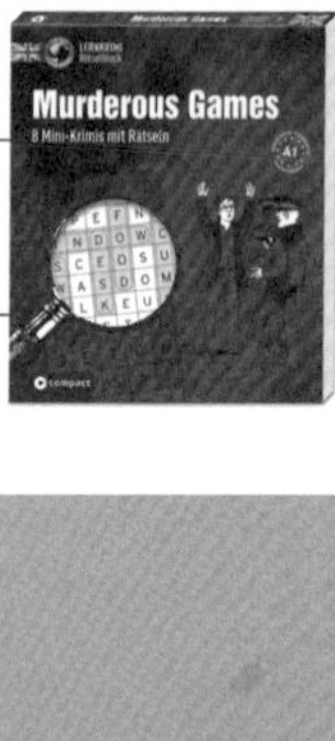

A2

The Art of Crime
ISBN 978-3-8174-1964-7

B1

A Deadly Puzzle
ISBN 978-3-8174-8832-2

Sprachtraining Englisch
Übung macht den Meister!

Gemeinsamer Europäischer Referenzrahmen A2/B1

144 Seiten
ISBN 978-3-8174-1764-3

Das Übungsbuch ist ideal für geübte Anfänger und Lerner mit mittlerem Sprachniveau, die ihre Englischkenntnisse auffrischen und vertiefen möchten. Rund 200 thematisch sortierte Übungen zu Wortschatz und Grammatik machen das Training abwechslungsreich und effektiv.

Infokästen erklären sprachliche und landeskundliche Besonderheiten. Lösungen und Glossar im Anhang.

Extra: Krimilektüre für geübte Anfänger – so wird das Sprachtraining noch spannender!

Gemeinsamer Europäischer Referenzrahmen A1/A2

Auch für Niveau A1-A2 erhältlich:
144 Seiten
ISBN 978-3-8174-1648-6